# JOHN QUINCY ADAMS
# 1767-1848

## Chronology Documents Bibliographical Aids

*Edited by*
**KENNETH V. JONES**

*Series Editor*
**HOWARD F. BREMER**

1970
OCEANA PUBLICATIONS, INC.
Dobbs Ferry, New York

Library of Congress Catalog Card Number: 71-111216
International Standard Book Number: 0-379-12073-9

Manufactured in the United States of America

# CONTENTS

# EDITOR'S FOREWORD

Every attempt has been made to cite the most accurate dates in this Chronology. Diaries, documents, letters, and similar evidence have been used to determine the exact date. If, however, later scholarship has found such dates to be obviously erroneous, the more plausible date has been used. Should this Chronology be in conflict with other authorities, the student is urged to go back to original sources as well as to such careful biographers as Arthur Stanley Link.

This is a research tool compiled primarily for the student. While it does make some judgments on the significance of the events, it is hoped that they are reasoned judgments based on a long acquaintance with American History.

Obviously, the very selection of events by any writer is itself a judgment.

The essence of these little books is in their making available some pertinent facts and key documents plus a critical bibliography which should direct the student to investigate for himself additional and/or contradictory material. The works cited may not always be available in small libraries, but neither are they usually the old, out of print, type of book often included in similar accounts.

# CHRONOLOGY

# CHRONOLOGY

## EARLY LIFE

### 1767

July 11 — Born in Braintree, Massachusetts (now Quincy). Father: John Adams, second President, a young Boston lawyer at this time. Mother: Abigail Smith, one of the most educated women in the colonies and daughter of an old and highly respected family.

### 1775

June 17 — Climbed Penn's Hill with Abigail to watch the battle of Bunker Hill, and the burning of Charlestown across the bay. Family doctor and friend, Joseph Warren, who had recently saved young John's leg from amputation, was killed in the battle. This made a lifelong impression on the young boy of eight.

### 1778

February 13 — Embarked on the American Frigate Boston with John Adams for France. John Adams was one of three commissioners to France, others were Benjamin Franklin and Arthur Lee.

Spring — Entered private boarding school where he studied French, Latin, dancing, music, fencing and drawing.

### 1779

August 3 — Returned to Boston with his Father.

November 15 — With younger brother Charles accompanied father to Spain. John Adams had been commisioned by Congress to negotiate a peace treaty with Great Britain.

### 1780

February 9 — After traveling in Spain during December and January the Adams threesome arrived in Paris. The boys resumed their studies.

Spring — John Adams appointed Minister to Netherlands. The two brothers attended public Latin school in Amsterdam and listened to lectures at the University of Leiden. John Q. also studied Dutch.

1

### 1781

July 7          At age 14 John Q. left for St. Petersburg as secre-
                tary to Francis Dana, recently appointed Minister
                to Russia.

August 29       Arrived at St. Petersburg for start of a 14-month
                stay. French Ambassador Marquis de Verac aided
                Dana in trying to convince Catherine the Great to
                recognize the new republic. Young John, who had
                mastered French, played a key role as Dana spoke
                no French and De Verac spoke no English.

### 1782

October         Left St. Petersburg for the Hague.

### 1783

April           Called to Paris by his father and was appointed one
                of his secretaries. Adams, Jay and Franklin headed
                a commission to draw up the treaties of peace and
                independence.

### 1785

January 1       Began his famous diary which he kept quite steadily
                to the end of his life.

May             Left Paris and returned to Quincy and began priv-
                ate study to prepare for Harvard.

### 1786

March           Admitted to Harvard as a member of the Junior
                class.

### 1787

July 16         Graduated from Harvard second in his class and
                a member of Phi Beta Kappa. Gave a graduation
                address on "The Importance and Necessity of Pub-
                lic Faith to the Well-Being of a Nation."

September       The graduation address was printed in the "Colum-
                bian Magazine" and became the subject of some
                newspaper criticism and controversy. Began a three
                year study of law under Theophilus Parsons of
                Newburyport, Massachusetts.

### 1790

July 15         Formally admitted to the practice of law in Massa-
                chusetts. Opened law office in Boston.

## 1791

July

Wrote "Letters of Publicola" which were printed in the "Columbian Centinel" of Boston. On the surface, the letters were a critique of Tom Paine's rights of man, but actually defended his father against the attacks of Jefferson.

## 1793

April 24

Began "Marcellus" articles calling for the neutrality of the United States in the British-French war. He argued that the change in French Government absolved the United States of treaty obligations. Articles comprised a sound defense of President Washington's position, and caught his attention and admiration.

November 30

Began writing "Columbus" articles that upheld George Washington in the Citizen Genet affair. The letters helped turn public opinion behind Washington, who once again was highly impressed with the young Boston lawyer.

# THE YOUNG DIPLOMAT

## 1794

May 20

Nominated by Washington as Minister to the Dutch Republic.

September 17

Left with younger brother Charles, who was appointed his secretary, for the Dutch Republic, but made a stop in London to deliver State papers to John Jay.

November 19

Jay's treaty signed. Sitting in on the final debates, Adams was aware of the United States surrender of the freedom of the seas. His later diplomatic career was often dedicated to regaining this principle.

December

Arrived in the Hague just as the old Dutch Republic fell to France. He soon became the listening post for his father and for Secretary of State Edmund Randolph.

## 1795

May 22

Wrote to father that "above all I wish we may never have any occasion for any political connections with Europe." Almost the identical words were used by

George Washington the following year in his Farewell Address.

November 11     Arrived in London to help in the final ratifications of the Jay treaty. Adams' diplomatic skills left much to be desired and he was easily handled by the British.

### 1796
May 28          Nominated by Washington as Minister Plenipotentiary to Portugal.

November        John Adams elected President of the United States.

### 1797
July 26         John Q. married Louisa Catherine Johnson, daughter of Joshua Johnson, Consul to London.

July            Received word that his father had changed his appointment from Portugal to Prussia.

November 7      Arrived with his bride and his brother Thomas in Berlin to begin duties as Minister Plenipotentiary to Prussia.

### 1799
July 11         On his 32nd birthday signed the Prussian-American Maritime Treaty.

### 1800
November        Jefferson elected president over John Adams.

November 30     Brother Charles Adams died.

Fall            France purchased Louisiana from Spain.

### 1801
February 3      Recalled from Prussia. Returned to the United States to resume law practice.

April 13        First son, George Washington Adams, born in Berlin.

### 1802
April           Elected to the Massachusetts State Senate.

November        Lost election to the House of Representatives from the Boston district by just 59 votes.

## SENATOR

### 1803

| | |
|---|---|
| February | Elected by the Federalists in the Massachusetts legislature to the United States Senate. Supported Federalists on most domestic issues, although regarded with suspicion by the Essex Junto, his father's opponents. |
| Summer | Purchased Old Penn's Hill farm from father for a home. |
| July 4 | Birth of second son, John. |
| October | Angered Federalists by supporting the Louisiana purchase. |

### 1804

| | |
|---|---|
| October 26 | Began series of four articles signed "Publius Valerius" which served to justify his anti-Federalist record in the Senate. |

### 1806

| | |
|---|---|
| February 5 | Helped draft resolutions complaining of British capture of American shipping. Advocated economic reprisal against Great Britain. He was the only Federalist in the Senate to vote for the nonimportation act. |
| Summer | Began lectures as Professor of Rhetoric and Oratory, at Harvard. |
| September | Received honorary Doctor of Law degree from Princeton. |

### 1807

| | |
|---|---|
| February | Adams made first public proposals for a Federal plan for internal improvement of roads, canals and waterways. The Senate quickly voted down the proposals with little or no discussion. |
| June 22 | Leopard-Chesapeake affair brought matters of Freedom of seas and British impressment to a head. Adams' support for the Administration led to his final split with the Federalists. |

August 18          The third and most famous of his sons, Charles
                   Francis Adams, was born.

December 18        Further infuriated the Federalists by voting for
                   Jefferson's Embargo act.

### 1808

January 23         Adams, by attending a Republican caucus, indicated
                   publicly his break with the Federalists.

March 15           Confidential interview with Jefferson convinced
                   Adams that the President, despite the Federalists
                   claim, had no secret plans with France to join her
                   in a war against England.

May                Federalists in the Massachusetts legislature elected
                   James Lloyd Jr. to succeed Adams in the United
                   States Senate. The election was six months early.

June 8             As soon as Adams learned of the premature elec-
                   tion of Lloyd, he resigned his seat.

## THE STATESMAN

### 1809

March 6            President Madison appointed Adams as Minister
                   Plenipotentiary to Russia.

April–June         Adams reviewed works of Fisher Ames in "Boston
                   Patriot," and once again antagonized the Federalists.

June 27            Senate confirmed Adams' appointment to Russia.

August 5           Adams, wife and young son leave for St. Petersburg.
                   Two oldest sons left with grandparents in Quincy.

### 1811

February           While still in Russia, Adams nominated and confirmed
                   by the Senate to the U.S. Supreme Court, but im-
                   mediately refused, believing himself unfit for the
                   position.

### 1812

June 18            American Congress voted to declare war on Great
                   Britain.

June 25            Napoleon invaded Russia.

### 1814

January 18         Adams named head of committee to discuss peace
                   with Great Britain at Ghent. Other committee mem-
                   bers were Albert Gallatin, James Bayard, Henry
                   Clay and John Russell.

August 8           Talks at Ghent commenced.

December 24        Treaty of Ghent ending war with Great Britain signed.

### 1815

January            Andrew Jackson defeated British in a "post war"
                   victory at New Orleans.

May 7              Adams appointed Minister Plenipotentiary to Great
                   Britain.

July 3             Adams, Clay and Gallatin signed Commercial Treaty
                   with Great Britain.

### 1816

January 25         Adams began negotiations with Lord Castlereagh for
                   reduction of naval armaments on the Great Lakes.
                   These early negotiations paved the way for the Rush-
                   Bagot Agreement which is largely responsible for
                   the lack of military establishments on the Canadian-
                   United States border today.

April 28-29        Rush-Bagot Agreement signed.

June 15            Adams left for home after being appointed Secre-
                   tary of State in James Monroe's cabinet.

## SECRETARY OF STATE

September 22       Adams sworn in as Secretary of State.

### 1818

July 15            Andrew Jackson's actions in Florida debated in
                   Cabinet Meeting. Adams was General Jackson's only
                   supporter.

October 20      Treaty between United States and Great Britain.
                Adams managed to keep Newfoundland fishing rights
                and the Northwest Boundary questions still favor-
                able to the United States, if not yet finally settled.

October 28      Adams saddened by the death of his mother, Abigail
                Adams, at the age of 74.

November 28     Adams sent communication to Spanish government in
                which he justified Jackson's violation of Spanish
                territory and demanded that Spain maintain order
                in Florida or cede it to the United States.

                              1819
February 22     Adams-Onis Treaty (Transcontinental Treaty)
                signed. Adams later called it the most important
                work of his life. It called for Spain to cede to the
                United States East and West Florida, and drew a
                transcontinental line, west of the Mississippi, that
                established United States' claims to the Oregon ter-
                ritory. Also submitted to the Senate his scholarly
                "Report on Weights and Measures," urging a stand-
                ard world-wide system, based on the metric system.

February 24     United States Senate unanimously ratified the Adams-
                Onis Treaty. Final acceptance, delayed by Spain,
                was on February 22, 1821.

                              1820
May 15          Monroe signed an act which closed United States
                ports against vessels coming from all British-
                American colonies.

                              1821
July 4          In an Independence Day oration, Adams called for
                American principles of Anti-Colonialism and non-
                intervention.

                              1822
February 15     Massachusetts legislature nominated John Quincy
                Adams for President.

March 8         President Monroe, in special message to Congress,
                recognized the new Latin American states. Congress
                voted $100,000 for missions to nations on the Amer-
                ican continent that the President deemed proper.

June 19 — Monroe signalized the first act of recognition of South American States by formally receiving Manuel Torres, Charge d'Affaires of Gran Columbia.

June 24 — Shipping treaty signed with France. England passed trade bill which allowed United States ships equal footing with British ships in West Indian ports.

August 24 — Presidential proclamation allowed British ships from West Indian ports to enter United States ports, but did not remove tonnage duty or importation taxes.

## 1823

March 1 — Congress passed British Trade bill which in effect called for equal footing with British vessels in any port in the British empire. Britain immediately issued an order-in-council which put a tonnage tax on American shipping. The British-American trade problems would return to haunt Adams during his administration.

March — France declared war on Spain, setting off chain of reaction that led to the Monroe Doctrine.

May 17 — Adams, in instructions to Caesar A. Rodney, Minister to the United Provinces of the Rio do la Plata, stated the United States support of republicanism in Latin America.

July — Made ill-advised business venture in purchase of Columbian Mills, a grist and flour mill in the District of Columbia. Its losses kept him in financial difficulties until late in his life.

October 9 — Unknown to Adams and Monroe, Great Britain had received assurances in the Polignac Memorandum that France would not intervene in Latin America.

November 7 — At Cabinet Meeting Adams turned down any British overtures for cooperative effort in Latin America; "It would be more candid, as well as more dignified, to avow our principles explicitly to Russia and France, than to come in as a cock-boat in the wake of a British Man-of-War."

December 2 — Monroe Doctrine announced to Congress in President's Annual Message. Secretary of State Adams played a huge part in its formation and most of the principles were his.

### 1824

January 8

On anniversary of Battle of New Orleans, Adams gave a ball for Andrew Jackson. Most important Washingtonians were present.

March 1

State convention at Harrisburg, Pennsylvania, nominated Andrew Jackson for President and John C. Calhoun for Vice President. This took Calhoun out of the presidential race.

March 15

Adams worked closely with Great Britain on the Slave Trade Convention. It would have effectively ended the trade, but the Convention was never ratified by the United States Senate.

May 22

Monroe signed the Tariff Act of 1824.

December 1

Presidential election returns indicated no winner in the electoral college. Jackson: 99 electoral votes and 155,872 popular votes. John Quincy Adams: 84 electoral votes and 105,321 popular votes. William Crawford: 41 electoral votes and 44,282 popular votes. Henry Clay: 37 electoral votes and 46,587 popular votes. The Constitution called for the outcome of the election to be settled in the House with each state receiving one vote. Henry Clay, with the smallest number of electoral votes had to withdraw, but he assumed important aspects in the making of the President. John C. Calhoun was easily elected Vice President, receiving 182 of the 261 electoral votes.

December 10

Robert P. Letcher of Kentucky, member of the House and close friend of Clay, called on Adams. During several other discussions between Letcher and Adams a meeting was arranged with Clay.

### 1825

January 9

Clay called on Adams and said he would support him in the House. Clay was confident when he left that he could have any seat in the cabinet he desired. All through the later charges of the Jacksonians of a corrupt deal, Secretary of State for the Presidency, Adams maintained that he made no such offer. However, his diary, which seldom neglects important events, is silent on this meeting. It would appear that the two men had some kind of understanding. (See Documents).

February 9    House of Representatives elected John Quincy Adams President on the first vote with a bare majority of 13 of the 24 states.

February 12   Adams offered position of Secretary of State to Clay. Clay asked for time to think it over, but accepted on February 18. The cabinet for the Tenth Administration was Henry Clay, Secretary of State; Richard Rush, Secretary of the Treasury; James Barbour, Secretary of War (replaced by Peter B. Porter in 1828); Samuel L. Southard, Secretary of Navy; William Wirt, Attorney General; and James McLean, Postmaster General. Other important appointments were: aged Federalist Rufus King, Minister to Great Britain; James Brown of Louisiana continued as Minister to France; Alexander Everett of Boston, Minister to Spain and Christopher Hughes as Charge d'Affairs at the Hague. Joel R. Poinsett was named the first Minister to Mexico.

March 3       Treaty of Indian Springs (Creeks) passed by Senate and later signed by Adams.

# PRESIDENT

March 4       John Quincy Adams inaugurated as the sixth president of the United States. His Inaugural Address called for an end to rancor and pleaded for national harmony (See Documents). His appointments, however, neglected the supporters of Jackson, Crawford and Calhoun.

June 13       Adams almost drowned while taking his regular morning swim in the Potamac river.

June 27       First of several British acts regulating the transfer of her West Indian colonies almost entirely shut off American trade. Adams' inability to stop the trade loss was effectively used against him in the 1828 campaign.

Late Summer    Spent what was to be his last summer with the aging John Adams in Quincy.

October 26    Erie Canal officially opened at Buffalo, New York. Completed a 544 mile inland water route from Buffalo to Albany on the canal, and down the Hudson River to New York.

October 30    Adams returned to Washington from summer vacation in Quincy.

November 2 & 3    Ministers of Columbia and Mexico invited the United States to send delegates to the Panama Congress.

December 5    John Taylor, Adams' selection, elected Speaker of the House by a slim two vote majority.

December 25    Commercial treaty signed with the Central American Republics.

December 26    Adams submitted the names of Richard C. Anderson of Kentucky and John Sergeant of Pennsylvania to Congress as envoys to the Panama Congress.

1826

January 6    First number of the United States Telegraph appeared in Washington. Edited by Duff Green, it became the spokesman for the Jacksonian forces.

January 24    Second treaty with Creeks signed. Creeks ceded all lands in Georgia except portions lying West of the Chattahoochee River, and the United States guaranteed to them such lands as were not ceded. The Creeks were given until January 1, 1827 to leave.

February 15    Van Buren introduced in the Senate two resolutions condemning the President for usurping the power of the Senate in accepting the invitation to the Panama Congress. Asked if Adams was going to make public all the messages and papers relating to the invitation.

February 16    In a message to the Senate Adams clearly pointed out that letters and messages dealing with the invitation to the Panama Congress were the business of the executive branch of government, and questioned the Senate's motives in asking about them.

| | |
|---|---|
| March 14 | Senate finally confirmed the appointments of Anderson and Sergeant as envoys to the Panama Congress. |
| March 15 | Adams asks House for money to send the envoys to Panama. |
| March 30 | John Randolph in Senate makes "Blifil and Black George" speech, referring contemptuously to Adams and Clay, "the Puritan and the Blackleg." Clay challenged Randolph to a duel. |
| April 8 | Randolph and Clay met on the Virginia bank of the Potomac. Fortunately neither was hurt. |
| April 22 | House appropriated $40,000 to send envoys to Panama Congress after much debate. Writing under the assumed name of Patrick Henry, Adams attacked Vice President Calhoun, in the "Washington National Journal," for allowing Randolph so much time in his speech. |
| May 9 | Appointed Robert Trimble of Kentucky to Supreme Court. |
| May 20 | Calhoun, writing under the assumed name Onslow, in the "National Intelligencer," answered Patrick Henry. |
| June 1 | Date named for the start of the Panama Congress. |
| June 7 | Once again Adams replied to Onslow. From now until late October the country watched the President and Vice President argue in the press. |
| July | Albert Gallatin left for England to replace Rufus King who had asked to be retired as U.S. Minister. Adams needed Gallatin's abilities to attempt to win back the West Indian Trade. |
| July 4 | John Adams and Thomas Jefferson died within hours of each other. |
| July 9 | John Q., on the way home for annual summer vacation, learned of father's death. |
| July 24 | Richard Anderson died on his way to the Panama Congress, and John Sergeant, who had asked for permission to delay his departure, didn't arrive |

until it was over, thus the United States was never represented.

September 1    Governor George M. Troup of Georgia disregarded the second Indian treaty, and sent surveyors into the Creek lands.

October 6      Adams left Quincy for Washington after arranging his father's estate.

November 13    Convention signed with Great Britain called for Great Britain to pay $1,204,960 to United States citizens in indemnities for carrying off slaves in the War of 1812.

### 1827

January 10     Tariff question raised by attempt by woolen interests of Northeast to raise duties. The bill, introduced on this date, passed the House on February 10, but lost in the Senate on March 1 by Vice President Calhoun's tie-breaking vote. Calhoun was now anti-protectionist, as the interests of his state and region seemed to require.

January 29     Adams wrote Governor Troup of Georgia, saying he would use force if necessary to back the Creek Indian Treaty.

February 2     Martin V. Mott decision of the Supreme Court gave president the final authority for calling out state militias.

February 5     In message to both Houses, Adams placed Georgia-Creek Indian problem before Congress.

February 17    In a letter to Secretary of War James Barbour, Governor Troup of Georgia said that Georgia would fight if federal troops entered the state over the Creek Indian question.

February 24    Senate voted 29 to 9 for an amendment to a British Trade bill for the purpose of blaming Adams and the Administration for losing the West Indian Trade. It was clear that Adams had lost complete control of the Senate.

March 2        Congress raised the salary of the Postmaster General to the same level as that of other cabinet heads.

March 17        Proclamation by Adams closed American ports to British vessels coming from any British colony in the Western Hemisphere.

May 5           Andrew Stevenson of Virginia was elected speaker of the House; Adams had lost control of both houses of Congress.

Summer          On advice of his doctor, Adams spent a full eleven week vacation in Quincy.

July 30         Delegates from 13 states, meeting in Harrisburg, Pennsylvania, demanded higher tariffs on raw wood and woolen goods.

August 6        Joint occupation of Oregon agreed to by the United States and Great Britain. Agreement was subject to termination on notice of one year.

November 15     Final Creek Treaty. Indians ceded all lands to Georgia and were moved across the Mississippi where many of them starved to death. (See Documents).

December 4      Adams' third annual message does not mention a protective tariff, thus offending many of the Administration supportors in Congress.

1828

February 28     John Adams II married his cousin, Mary Helen, in White House wedding.

April 8         John Adams II insulted Russell Jarvis, editorial writer for the "Daily Telegram," and it took the full cabinet to prevent a duel.

May 19          Tariff of Abominations passed by Congress and signed by Adams (at this time the President felt he could use the veto power only if he thought a bill was unconstitutional). Even though the Jacksonians may have been fooled when the bill passed, it proved the instrument for making Jackson the next president.

May 24          Congress authorized President to remove by proclamation any duties levied on goods imported by foreign ships for any nation which will do the same for United States shipping.

July 4            Adams broke ground in Baltimore for the construc-
                  tion of the Baltimore and Ohio Railroad which, in
                  1830, was to become the first passenger railroad to
                  begin operations.

Summer-Fall       Renominated for President by several state legis-
                  latures. The old system of nominations by congres-
                  sional caucus was now obsolete. Richard Rush of
                  Pennsylvania, Secretary of the Treasury, was nomin-
                  ated for Vice President. Jackson's supporters, of
                  course, nominated the General, with John C. Cal-
                  houn of South Carolina as his running mate.

                  The elements of the two rival political parties were
                  now completed. The Adams-Clay faction would soon
                  be labelled as National Republicans or Whigs. The
                  Jackson-Calhoun-Van Buren forces were beginning
                  to call themselves Democrats.

                  Presidential Campaign marked by lies and slander
                  against both candidates and their wives. Adams
                  failed to reprove his followers for their vicious
                  attacks on Rachel Jackson. Neither candidate cam-
                  paigned formally.

October 31 –      Jackson defeated Adams for reelection: 178 elec-
November 14       toral votes to 83. Popular votes stood at 647,276
                  for Jackson, and 508,065 votes for Adams.

December 2        Granddaughter, Mary Louisa, born to the John
                  Adams II's.

December 22       Death of Rachel Jackson completed the split be-
                  tween Adams and Andrew Jackson.


## CONGRESSMAN

### 1829

March 3           Adams moved out of White House to a home on
                  Meriden Hill in Washington which he rented from
                  David Porter.

March 4           Inauguration of Andrew Jackson. Adams did not at-
                  tend (just as his father had refused to attend the
                  inauguration of Thomas Jefferson).

| | |
|---|---|
| April 30 | Oldest son George Washington Adams drowned by accident or suicide in Long Island Sound. |
| June | Adams returns to Quincy to begin retirement. |
| September 3 | Charles Francis Adams married Abigail Brooks, daughter of Peter Brooks, a wealthy insurance man of Boston. |
| November 24 | George Washington Adams' remains are brought to Quincy by sea. Buried in the family supulcher. |
| December 5 | Adams rejoined wife in son John's home in Washington. |

## 1830

| | |
|---|---|
| January 8 | Invited to Jackson Day Dinner in Washington, but preferred to remain at home. |
| Summer | Adams, Louisa, Mary Helen Adams and grandaughter return to Quincy. |
| September 18 | The Reverend Joseph Richardson and John Davis, both Massachusetts Congressmen, asked Adams if he would serve in the House of Representatives if elected. Adams said he would. |
| October 12 | Delegates from 13 towns in the Plymouth District met in the village of Halifax and nominated Adams for the House of Representatives. |
| November 1 | Adams elected to House by a large majority. |

## 1831

| | |
|---|---|
| March 4 | Adams took his seat in the House of Representatives where he served for the rest of his life (1830 to 1848). |
| Spring | Returned for summer to Quincy. |
| August 13 | Granddaughter, Louisa Catherine, born to Charles Francis. |

September 26    Anti-Mason Party meeting at Baltimore did not (as
he hoped it might) nominate John Quincy Adams as
its candidate for President. Adams was a fervent
Anti-Mason.

### 1832

July 11         By refusing to vote on a resolution to censor a
member, Adams set a precedent that allows a minority to defeat a majority by refusing to vote —
thus preventing a quorum.

### 1833

September 23    John Quincy Adams II, first grandson to carry on
name, born to Charles Francis Adams.

November 1      Adams, running for Governor of Massachusetts on
the Anti-Mason ticket, ran second to John Davis.
Although there was no majority, Adams withdrew
from the race.

### 1834

October 23      Death of second son, John Adams II.

### 1835

December 17     $500,000 left for Smithsonian Institute by James
Smithson. Adams served as chairman, for ten years,
of the House committee to handle the fund.

### 1836

January 22      Adams' speech in the House answered Webster's
in the Senate on the fortification bill. This speech
is given credit for destroying Webster's chance to
succeed to the White House.

May 19          Gag rule went into effect for the first time over
Adams' objections and vote. Adams began eight
year fight to rescind it.

### 1838

February 16     Grandson Henry Adams born, son of Charles Francis.

### 1839

August 26       L'Amistad, a vessel whose slave cargo had revolted,
was brought into New London by the U.S.S. Washing-
ton.

December                 Adams organized the House and was placed in the
                         Speaker's chair for ten days after the House clerk
                         had held up organization for four days by refusing
                         to call the role.


                                      1841
March 9                  United States Supreme Court freed Negroes of
                         L'Amistad after Adams placed their appeal before
                         it.


                                      1842
January 25               Adams presented a petition to dissolve the Union,
                         and the House started a censor trial.

February 9               Motion to censor Adams tabled.


                                      1843
October 28               Adams left on a hard winter trip to make a corner-
                         stond address for the observatory of the Cincinnati
                         Astronomical Society.

November 23              Reached Quinoy completely exhausted after the
                         month-long trip to Cincinnati.


                                      1845
December 3               Gag rule was finally rescinded by a vote in the
                         House of Representatives of 108 to 80. This was
                         Adams' greatest victory in the House as it was
                         the end of an eight year fight against the Southern
                         slave interests.


                                      1846
April 28                 Adams' arguments helped influence Congress to pass
                         a bill on the Smithsonian bequest. The House had
                         been handling the bequest for over ten years, but
                         it had never officially accepted it.

June 15                  Oregon boundary settled as Adams lived to see his
                         dreams of Northwest expansion come true.

August                   Adams returned to Qunicy for the summer.

November 10              People of his district reelected him to Congress by
                         a large majority.

November 20        Adams collapsed on an inspection tour of the new
                   medical college at Harvard.

## 1847

February 8         Almost completely recovered, left for Washington
                   and was in his seat by February 13. Friends and
                   enemies alike arose to applaud him as he took his
                   seat.

Summer             Back in Quincy for the last vacation.

July 11            Quietly celebrated his 81st birthday.

July 27            Small family gathering helped Adams and Louisa
                   celebrate their 50th wedding anniversary.

December 6         Returned to Washington and took his seat in Con-
                   gress.

## 1848

February 21        Adams collapsed at his seat in the House of Repre-
                   sentatives.

February 23        Adams died after lying in a coma for two days. Last
                   reported words were, "This is the last of earth —
                   I am content."

February 25        Services held in the House of Representatives.

March 11           Adams interred in family tomb in Quincy.

## 1852

May 15             Louisa Adams died. After bringing his mother's
                   body home from Washington, Charles Francis Adams
                   had the remains of his father transferred along
                   with those of Louisa, John, and Abigail to a granite
                   crypt beneath the church portal at Quincy.

# DOCUMENTS

# DOCUMENTS

## DIARY COMMENTS ON HENRY CLAY'S VISIT
### January 9, 1825

*Adams said nothing about a deal with Clay — presidency for secretary of state. Yet, the diary which is usually full of details on important events is extremely bare of details in the accounting of this meeting — and a blank space left to be filled in later, never was.*

January 9, 1825 ... Mr. Clay came at six, and spent the evening with me in a long conversation explanatory of the past and prospective of the future. He said that the time was drawing near when the choice must be made in the House of Representatives of a President from the three candidates presented by the electoral colleges; that he had been much urged and solicited with regard to the part in that trans-action that he should take, and had not been five minutes landed at his lodgings before he had been applied to by a friend of Mr. Craw-ford's, in a manner so gross that it had disgusted him; that some of my friends also, disclaiming, indeed, to have any authority from me, had repeatedly applied to him, directly or indirectly, urging consid-erations personal to himself motives to his cause. He had thought it best to reserve for some time his determination to himself; first, to give a decent time for his own funeral solemnities as a candidate; and, secondly, to prepare and predispose all his friends to a state of neutrality between the three candidates who would be before the House, so that they might be free ultimately to take that course which might be most conducive to the public interest. The time had now come at which he might be explicit in his communication with me, and he had for that purpose asked this confidential interview. He wished me, as far as I might think proper, to satisfy him with regard to some prin-ciples of great public importance, but without any personal consider-ations for himself. In the question to come before the House between General Jackson, Mr. Crawford, and myself, he had no hesitation in saying that his preference would be for me.

## INAUGURAL ADDRESS
### March 4, 1825

*Because he was quite conscious of his role as a minority president Adams was quite humble in his address. He asked for national unity, internal improvements and the aid of Congress.*

In compliance with an usage coeval with the existence of our Federal Constitution, and sanctioned by the example of my predecessors in the career upon which I am about to enter, I appear, my fellow-citizens, in your presence and in that of Heaven to bind myself by the solemnities of religious obligation to the faithful performance of the duties allotted to me in the station to which I have been called.

In unfolding to my countrymen the principles by which I shall be governed in the fullfillment of those duties my first resort will be to that Constitution which I shall swear to the best of my ability to preserve, protect and defend. That revered instrument enumerates the powers and prescribes the duties of the Executive Magistrate and in its first words declares the purposes to which these and the whole action of the Government instituted by it should be invariably and sacredly devoted – to form a more perfect union, establish justice, insure domestic tranquillity, provide for the common defense, promote the general welfare, and secure the blessings of liberty to the people of this Union in their successive generations. Since the adoption of this social compact one of these generations has passed away. It is the work of our forefathers. Administered by some of the most eminent men who contributed to its formation, through a most eventful period in the annals of the world, and through all the vicissitudes of peace and war incidental to the conditions of associated man, it has not disappointed the hopes and aspirations of those illustrious benefactors of their age and nation. It has promoted the lasting welfare of that country so dear to us all; it has to an extent far beyond the ordinary lot of humanity secured the freedom and happiness of this people. We now receive it as a precious inheritance from those to whom we are indebted for its establishment, doubly bound by the examples which they have left us and by the blessings which we have enjoyed as the fruits of their labors to transmit the same unimpaired to the succeeding generations.

In the compass of thirty-six years since this great national covenant was instituted a body of laws enacted under its authority and in conformity with its provisions has unfolded its powers and carried into practical operation its effective energies. Subordinate departments have distributed the executive functions in their various relations to foreign affairs, to the revenue and expenditures, and to the military force of the Union by land and sea. A coordinate department of the judiciary has expounded the Constitution and the laws, settling in harmonious coincidence with the legislative will numerous weighty questions of construction which the imperfection of human language had rendered unavoidable. The year of jubilee since the first formation of our Union has just elapsed; that of the declaration of our independence is at hand. This consummation of both was effected by this Constitution.

Since that period a population of four millions has multiplied to twelve. A territory bounded by the Mississippi has been extended from sea to sea. New States have been admitted to the Union in numbers nearly equal to those of the first Confederation. Treaties of peace, amity, and commerce have been concluded with the principal dominions of the earth. The people of other nations, inhabitants of regions acquired not by conquest, but by compact, have been united with us in the participation of our rights and duties, of our burdens and blessings. The forest has fallen by the ax of our woodsmen; the soil has been made to teem by the tillage of our farmers; our commerce has whitened every ocean. The dominion of man over physical nature has been extended by the invention of our artists. Liberty and law have marched hand in hand. All the purposes of human association have been accomplished as effectively as under any other government on the globe, and at a cost little exceeding in a whole generation the expenditure of other nations in a single year.

Such is the unexaggerated picture of our condition under a Constitution founded upon the republican principle of equal rights. To admit that this picture has its shades is but to say that it is still the condition of men upon earth. From evil — physical, moral, and political — it is not our claim to be exempt. We have suffered sometimes by the visitation of Heaven through disease; often by the wrongs and injustice of other nations, even to the extremities of war; and lastly, by dissensions among ourselves — dissensions perhaps inseparable from the enjoyment of freedom, but which have more than once appeared to threaten the dissolution of the Union, and with it the overthrow of all the enjoyments of our present lot and all our earthly hopes of the future. The causes of these dissensions have been various, founded upon differences of speculation in the theory of republican government; upon conflicting views of policy in our relations with foreign nations; upon jealousies of partial and sectional interests, aggravated by prejudices and prepossessions which strangers to each other are ever apt to entertain.

It is a source of gratification and of encouragement to me to observe that the great result of this experiment upon the theory of human rights has at the close of that generation by which it was formed been crowned with success equal to the most sanguine expectations of its founders. Union, justice tranquillity, the common defense, the general welfare, and the blessings of liberty — all have been promoted by the Government under which we have lived. Standing at this point of time,

looking back to that generation which has gone by and forward to that
which is advancing, we may at once indulge in grateful exultation and
in cheering hope. From the experience of the past we derive instruc-
tive lessons for the future. Of the two great political parties which have
divided the opinions and feelings of our country, the candid and the
just will now admit that both have contributed splendid talents, spot-
less integrity, ardent patriotism, and disinterested sacrifices to the
formation and administration of this Government, and that both have
required a liberal indulgence for a portion of human infirmity and
error. The revolutionary wars of Europe, commencing precisely at
the moment when the Government of the United States first went into
operation under this Constitution, excited a collision of sentiments and
of sympathies which kindled all the passions and imbittered the conflict of parties till the nation was involved in war and the Union was
shaken to its center. This time of trial embraced a period of five and
twenty years, during which the policy of the Union in its relations with
Europe constituted the principal basis of our political divisions and the
most arduous part of the action of our Federal Government. With the
catastrophe in which the wars of the French Revolution terminated,
and our own subsequent peace with Great Britain, this baneful weed of
party strife was uprooted. From that time no difference of principle,
connected either with the theory of government or with out intercourse
with foreign nations, has existed or been called forth in force sufficient to sustain a continued combination of parties or to give more
than wholesome animation to public sentiment or legislative debate.
Our political creed is, without a dissenting voice that can be heard,
that the will of the people, the source and the happiness of the people,
the end of all legitimate government upon the earth; that the best
security for the beneficience and the best guaranty against the abuse
of power consists in the freedom, the purity, and frequency of popular
elections; that the General Government of the Union and the separate
governments of the States are all sovereignties of limited powers,
fellow-servants of the same masters, uncontrolled within their respective sphere, uncontrollable by encroachments upon each other; that
firmest security of peace is the preparation during peace of the de-
fenses of war; that a rigorous economy and accountability of public
expenditures should guard against the aggravation and alleviate when
possible the burden of taxation; that the military should be kept in
strict subordination to the civil power; that the freedom of the press
and of religious opinion should be inviolate; that the policy of our
country is peace and the ark of our salvation union are articles of
faith upon which we are all now agreed. If there have been those who
doubted whether a confederated representative democracy were a
government competent to the wise and orderly management of the
common concerns of a mighty nation, those doubts have been dispelled;
if there have been projects of partial confederacies to be erected upon
the ruins of the Union, they have been scattered to the winds; if there
have been dangerous attachments to one foreign nation and antipathies

against another, they have been extinguished. Ten years of peace, at home and abroad, have assuaged the animosities of political contention and blended into harmony the most discordant elements of public opinion. There still remains one effort of magnamimity, one sacrifice of prejudice and passion, to be made by the individuals throughout the nation who have heretofore followed the standards of political party. It is that of discarding every remnant of rancor against each other, of embracing as countrymen and friends, and of yielding to talents and virtue alone that confidence which in times of contention for principle was bestowed only upon those who bore the badge of party communion.

The collisions of party spirit which originate in speculative opinions or in different views of administrative policy are in their nature transitory. Those which are founded on geographical divisions, adverse interest of soil, climate and modes of domestic life are more permanent, and therefore, perhaps, more dangerous. It is this which gives inestimable value to the character of our Government, at once federal and national. It holds out to us a perpetual admonition to preserve alike and with equal anxiety the rights of each individual State in its own government and the rights of the whole nation in that of the Union. Whatsoever is of domestic concernment, unconnected with the other members of the Union or with foreign lands, belongs exclusively to the administration of the State governments. Whatsoever directly involves the rights and interests of the federative fraternity or of foreign powers is of the resort of this General Government. The duties of both are obvious in the general principle, though sometimes perplexed with difficulties in the detail. To respect the rights of the State governments is the inviolable duty of that of the Union; the government of every State will feel its own obligation to respect and preserve the rights of the whole. The prejudices everywhere too commonly entertained against distant strangers are worn away, and the jealousies of jarring interests are allayed by the composition and functions of the great national councils annually assembled from all quarters of the Union at this place. Here the distinguished men from every section of our country, while meeting to deliberate upon the great interests of those by whom they are deputed, learn to estimate the talents and do justice to the virtures of each other. The harmony of the nation is promoted and the whole Union is knit together by the sentiments of mutual respect, the habits of social intercourse, and the ties of personal friendship formed between the representatives of its several parts in the performance of their service at this metropolis.

Passing from this general review of the purposes and injunctions of the Federal Constitution and their results as indicating the first traces of the path of duty in the discharge of my public trust, I return to the Administration of my immediate predecessor as the second. It has passed away in a period of profound peace, how much to the satisfaction of our country and to the honor of our country's name is known to you all. The great features of its policy, in general concurrence with the will of the Legislature, have been to cherish peace while preparing for defensive war; to yield exact justice to other nations and maintain the rights of our own; to cherish the principles of freedom and of equal rights wherever they were proclaimed; to discharge with all possible promptitude the national dept; to improve the organization and discipline of the Army; to provide and sustain a school of military science; to extend equal protection to all the great interests of the nation; to promote the civilization of the Indian tribes, and to proceed in the great system of internal improvements within the limits of the Constitutional power of the Union. Under the pledge of these promises, made by that eminent citizen at the time of his first induction to this office, in his career of eight years the internal taxes have been repealed; sixty millions of the public dept have been discharged; provision has been made for the comfort and relief of the aged and indigent among the surviving warriors of the Revolution; the regular armed force has been reduced and its constitution revised and perfected; the accountability for the expenditure of public moneys has been made more effective; the Floridas have been peaceably acquired, and our boundary has been extended to the Pacific Ocean; the independence of the southern nations of this hemisphere has been recognized, and recommended by example and by counsel to the potentates of Europe; progress has been made in the defense of the country by fortifications and the increase of the Navy, toward the effectual supression of the African traffic in slaves, in alluring the aboriginal hunters of our land to the cultivation of the soil and of the mind, in exploring the interior regions of the Union, and in preparing by scientific researches and surveys for the further application of our national resources to the internal improvement of our country.

In this brief outline of the promise and performance of my immediate predecessor the line of duty for his successor is clearly delineated. To pursue to their consummation those purposes of improvement in our common condition instituted or recommended by him will embrace the whole sphere of my obligations. To the topic of internal improvement, emphatically urged by him at his inauguration, I recur with peculiar satisfaction. It is that from which I am convinced that the unborn millions of our posterity who are in future ages to people this continent will derive their most fervent gratitude to the founders of the Union; that in which the beneficent action of its Government will be most deeply felt and acknowledged. The magnificence and splendor of their public works are among the imperishable glories of the ancient republics. The roads and aqueducts of Rome have been the admiration of all after ages, and have survived thousands of years after all her conquests have been swallowed up in despotism or become the spoil of barbarians. Some diversity of opinion has prevailed with regard to the powers of Congress for legislation upon objects of this nature. The most respectful deference is due to doubts originating in pure patriotism and sustained by venerated authority. But nearly twenty years have passed since the construction of the first national road was commenced. The authority for its construction was then unquestioned. To how many thousands of our countrymen has it proved a benefit?     To what single individual has it ever proved an injury? Repeated, liberal, and candid discussions in the Legislature have conciliated the sentiments and approximated the opinions of enlightened minds upon the question of constitutional power. I can not but hope that by the same process of friendly, patient and perservering deliveration all constitutional objections will ultimately be removed. The extent and limitations of the powers of the General Government in relation to this transcendently important interest will be settled and acknowledged to the common satisfaction of all, and every speculative scruple will be solved by a practical public blessing.

Fellow-citizens, you are acquainted with the peculiar circumstances of the recent election, which have resulted in affording me the opportunity of addressing you at this time. You have heard the exposition of the principles which will direct me in the fulfillment of the high and solemn trust imposed upon me in this station. Less possessed of your confidence in advance than any of my predecessors, I am deeply conscious of the prospect that I shall stand more and oftener in need of your indulgence. Intentions upright and pure, a heart devoted to the welfare of our country, and the unceasing application of all the faculties allotted to me to her service are all the pledges that I can give for the faithful performance of the arduous duties I am to undertake. To the guidance of the legislative councils, to the assistance of the executive and subordinate departments, to the friendly cooperation of the respective State governments, to the candid and liberal support of the people so far as it may be deserved by honest industry and zeal, I shall look for whatever success may attend my public service; and knowing that "except the Lord keep the city the watchman waketh but in vain," with fervent supplications for His favor, to His overruling providence I commit with humble but fearless confidence my own fate and the future destinies of my country.

# FIRST ANNUAL MESSAGE
## December 6, 1825

*In this message Adams put forward all his hopes for in-
ternal improvement — construction of national highways,
canals, a federal university, and a national observatory.
However, little or none of his progressive programs ever
received the backing of the Jacksonian Congress.*

Fellow-Citizens of the Senate and of the House of Representatives:

In taking a general survey of the concerns of our beloved country,
with references to subjects interesting to the common welfare, the
first sentiment which impresses itself upon the mind is of gratitude
to the Omnipotent Disposer of All Good for the continuance of the
signal blessings of His providence, and especially for that health which
to an unusual extent has prevailed within our borders, and for that
abundance which in the vicissitudes of the seasons has been scattered
with profusion over our land. There has, indeed, rarely been a period
in the history of civilized man in which the general condition of the
Christian nations has been marked so extensively by peace and prosperity.

Europe, with a few partial and unhappy exceptions, has enjoyed
ten years of peace, during which all her Governments, whatever the
theory of their constitutions may have been, are successively taught
to feel that the end of their institution is the happiness of the people,
and that the exercise of power among men can be justified only by the
blessings it confers upon those over whom it is extended. During the
same period our intercourse with all those nations has been pacific
and friendly; it so continues. Since the close of your last session no
material variation has occurred in our relations with any one of them.
In the commercial and navigation system of Great Britain important
changes of municipal regulations have recently been sanctioned by
acts of Parliament, the effect of which upon the interests of other
nations, and particularly upon ours, has not yet been fully developed.
In the recent renewal of the diplomatic missions on both sides between
the two Governments assurances have been given and received by the
continuance and increase of the mutual confidence and cordiality by
which the adjustment of many points of difference had already been
effected, and which affords the surest pledge for the ultimate satisfactory adjustment of those which still remain open or may hereafter
arise.

The policy of the United States in their commercial intercourse
with other nations has always been of the most liberal character. In
the mutual exchange of their respective productions they have abstained
altogether from prohibitions; they have interdicted themselves the
power of laying taxes upon exports, and whenever they have favored
their own shipping by special preferences or exclusive privileges in

their own ports it has been only with a view to countervail similar favors and exclusions granted by the nations with whom we have been engaged in traffic to their own people or shipping, and to the disadvantage of ours. Immediately after the close of the last war a proposal was fairly made by the act of Congress of the 3d of March, 1815, to all the maritime nations to lay aside the system of retanating restrictions and exclusions, and to place the shipping of both parties to the common trade on a footing of equality in respect to the duties of tonnage and impost. This offer was partially and successively accepted by Great Britain, Sweden, the Netherlands, the Hanseatic cities, Prussia, Sardinia, the Duke of Oldenburg, and Russia. It was also adopted, under certain modifications, in our late commercial convention with France, and by the act of Congress of 8th January, 1824, it has received a new confirmation with all nations who had acceded to it, and has been offered again to all those who are or may hereafter be willing to abide in reciprocity by it. But all these regulations, whether established by treaty or by municipal enactments, are still subject to one important restriction. The removal of discriminating duties of tonnage and of impost is limited to articles of the growth, produce or manufacture of the country to which the vessel belongs or to such articles as are must usually first shipped from her ports....

It is with great satisfaction that I am enabled to bear witness to the liberal spirit with which the Republic of Colombia has made satisfaction for well-established claims of a similar character, and among the documents now communicated to Congress will be distinguished a treaty of commerce and navigation with that Republic, the ratification of which have been exchanged since the last recess of the Legislature. The negotiation of similar treaties with all the independent South American States has been contemplated and may yet be accomplished. The basis of them all, as proposed by the United States, has been laid in two principles — the one of entire and unqualified reciprocity, the other the mutual obligation of the parties to place each other permanently upon the footing of the most favored nation....

Among the measures which have been suggested to them by the new relations with one another, resulting from the recent changes in their condition, is that of assembling at the Isthmus of Panama a congress at which each of them should be represented, to deliberate upon objects important to the welfare of all. The Republics of Colombia, of Mexico, and of Central America have already deputed plenipotentiaries to such a meeting, and they have invited the United States to be also represented there by their ministers. The invitation has been accepted, and ministers on the part of the United States will be commissioned to attend at those deliberations, and to take part in them so far as may be compatible with that neutrality from which it is neither our intention nor the desire of the other American States that we should depart....

The act of Congress of the 3d of March last, directing the Secretary of the Treasury to subscribe, in the name and for the use of the United States, for 1,500 shares of the capital stock of the Chesapeake and Delaware Canal Company, has been executed by the actual subscription for the amount specified: And such other measures have been adopted by that officer, under the act, as the fulfillment of its intentions requires. The latest accounts received of this important undertaking authorize the belief that it is in successful progress.

The payments into the Treasury from the proceeds of the sales of the public lands during the present year were estimated at $1,000,000. The actual receipts of the first two quarters have fallen very little short of that sum; it is not expected that the second half of the year will be equally productive, but the income of the year from that source may now be safely estimated at a million and a half. The act of Congress of 18th May, 1824, to provide for the extinguishment of the debt due to the United States by the purchasers of public lands, was limited in its operation of relief to the purchaser to the 10th of April last. Its effect at the end of the quarter during which it expired was to reduce that debt from ten to seven millions. By the operation of similar prior laws of relief, from and since that of 2d March, 1821, the debt has been reduced from upward of twenty-two millions to ten. It is exceedingly desirable that it should be extinguished altogether; and to facilitate that consummation I recommend to Congress the revival for one year more of the act of 18th May, 1824, with such provisional modification as may be necessary to guard the public interest against fraudulent practices in the resale of the relinquished land. The purchasers of public lands are among the most useful of our fellow-citizens, and since the system of sales for cash alone has been introduced great indulgence has been justly extended to those who had previously purchased upon credit. The debt which had been contracted under the credit sales had become unwieldy, and its extinction was alike advantageous to the purchaser and to the public. Under the system of sales, matured as it has been by experience, and adapted to the exigencies of the times, the lands will continue as they have become, an abundant source of revenue; and when the pledge of them to the public creditor shall have been redeemed by the entire discharge of the national debt, the swelling tide of wealth with which they replenish the common Treasury may be made to reflow in unfailing streams of improvement from the Atlantic to the Pacific Ocean.

The condition of the various branches of the public service resorting from the Department of War, and their administration during the current year, will be exhibited in the report of the Secretary of War and the accompanying documents herewith communicated. The organization and discipline of the Army are effective and satisfactory. To counteract the prevalence of desertion among the troops it has been suggested to withhold from the men a small portion of their monthly pay until the period of their discharge; and some expedient appears to be necessary to preserve and maintain among the officers so much of the art of horsemanship as could scarcely fail to be found wanting on the possible sudden eruption of a war, which should take us unprovided with a single corps of cavalry. The Military Academy at West Point, under the restrictions of a severe but paternal superintendence, recommends itself more and more to the patronage of the nation, and the numbers of meritorious officers which it forms and introduces to the public improvements to which their acquirements at that institution are peculiarly adapted. The school of artillery practice established at Fortress Monroe is well suited to the same purpose, and may need the aid of further legislative provision to the same end. The reports of the various officers at the head of the administrative branches of the military service, connected with the quartering, clothing, subsistence, health and pay of the Army, exhibit the assidous vigilance of those officers in the performance of their respective duties, and the faithful accountability which has pervaded every part of the system.

Our relations with the numerous tribes of aboriginal natives of this country, scattered over its extensive surface and so dependent even for their existence upon our power, have been during the present year highly interesting. An act of Congress of 25th of May, 1824, made an appropriation to defray the expenses of making treaties of trade and friendship with the Indian tribes beyond the Mississippi. An act of 3d of March 1825, authorized treaties to be made with the Indians for their consent to the making of a road from the frontier of Missouri to that of New Mexico, and another act of the same date provided for defraying the expenses of holding treaties with the Sioux, Chippeways, Menomenees, Sauks, Foxes, etc., for the purpose of establishing boundaries and promoting peace between said tribes. The first and the last objects of these acts have been accomplished, and the second is yet in process of execution. The treaties which since the last session of Congress have been concluded with the several tribes will be laid before the Senate for their consideration conformably to the Constitution. They comprise large and valuable acquisitions of territory, and they secure an adjustment of boundaries and give pledges of permanent peace between several tribes which had been long waging bloody wars against each other.

On the 12th of February last a treaty was signed at Indian Springs between commissioners appointed on the part of the United States and certain chiefs and individuals of the Creek Nation of Indians, which was received at the seat of Government only a very few days before the close of the last session of Congress and of the late Administration. The advice and consent of the Senate was given to it on the 3d of March, too late for it to receive the ratification of the then President of the United States; it was ratified on the 7th of March, under the unsuspecting impression that it had been negotiated in good faith and in the confidence inspired by the recommendation of the Senate.

The subsequent transaction in relation to this treaty will form the subject of a separate communication.

The appropriations made by Congress for public works, as well in the construction of fortifications as for purposes of internal improvement so far as they have been expended, have been faithfully applied. Their progress has been delayed by the want of suitable officers for superintending them. An increase of both the corps of engineers, military and topographical was recommended by my predecessor at the last session of Congress. The reasons upon which that recommendation was founded subsists in all their force and have acquired additional urgency since that time. It may also be expedient to organize the topographical engineers into a corps similar to the present establishment of the Corps of Engineers. The Military Academy at West Point will furnish from the cadets annually graduated there officers well qualified for carrying this measure into effect.

The Board of Engineers for Internal Improvement, appointed for carrying into execution the act of Congress of 30th of April, 1824, "to procure the necessary surveys, plans, and estimates on the subject of roads and canals," have been actively engaged in that service from the close of the last session of Congress. They have completed the surveys necessary for ascertaining the practicability of a canal from the Chesapeake Bay to the Ohio River, and are preparing a full report on that subject, which, when completed, will be laid before you. The same observation is to be made with regard to the two other objects of national Importance upon which the Board have been occupied, namely, the accomplishment of a national road from this city to New Orleans, and the practicability of uniting the waters of Lake Memphramagog with Connecticut River and the improvement of the navigation of that river. The surveys have been made and are nearly completed. The report may be expected at an early period during the present session of Congress.

The acts of Congress of the last session relative to the surveying, marking, or laying out roads in the Territories of Florida, Arkansas, and Michigan from Missouri to Mexico, and for the continuation of the Cumberland road, are, some of them, fully executied, and others in the process of execution. Those for completing or commencing fortifications have been delayed only so far as the Corps of Engineers has been inadequate to furnish officers for the necessary superintendence of the works. Under the act confirming the statutes of Virginia and Maryland incorporating the Chesapeake and Ohio Canal Company, three commissioners on the part of the United States have been appointed for opening books and receiving subscriptions, in concert with a like number of commissioners appointed on the part of each of those States. A meeting of the commissioners has been postponed, to await the definitive report of the board of engineers. The light-houses and monuments for the safety of our commerce and mariners, the works for the security of Plymouth Beach and for the preservation of the islands in Boston Harbor, have received the attention required by laws relating to those objects respectively. The continuation of the Cumberland road, the most important of them all, after surmounting no inconsiderable difficult in fixing upon the direction of the road, has commenced under the most promising asuspices, with the improvements of recent invention in the mode of construction, and with the advantage of a great reduction in the comparative cost of the work....

The objects of the West India Squadron have been to carry into execution the laws for suppression of the African slave trade; for the protection against open and unequivocal pirates. These objects during the present year have been accomplished more effectually than at any former period. The African slave trade has long been excluded from the use of our flag, and if some few citizens of our country have continued to set the laws of the Union as well as those of nature and humanity at defiance by persevering in that abominable traffic it has been only by shelterting themselves under the banners of other nations less earnest for the total extinction of the trade than ours. The irregular privateers have within the last year been in a great measure banished from those seas, and the pirates for months past appear to have been almost entirely swept away from the borders and the shores of the two Spanish islands in those regions....

It were, indeed, a vain and dangerous illusion to believe that in the present or probable condition of human society a commerce so extensive and so rich as ours could exist and be pursued in safety without the continual support of a military marine – the only arm by which the power of this Confederacy can be estimated or felt by foreign nations, and the only standing military force which can never be dangerous to our own liberties at home. A permanent naval peace establishment, therefore, adapted to our present condition, and adaptable to that gigantic growth with which the nation is advancing in its career, is among the subjects which have already occupied the foresight of the last Congress, and which will deserve your serious deliverations. Our Navy, commenced at an early period of our present political organization upon a scale commensurate with the incipient energies, the scanty resources, and the comparative indigence of our infancy, was even than found adequate to cope with all the powers of Barbary, save the first, and with one of the principal maritime powers of Europe.

At a period of further advancement, but with little accession of strength, it not only sustained with honor the most unequal of conflicts but covered itself and our country with unfading glory. But it is only since the close of the late war that by the numbers and force of the ships of which it was composed it could deserve the name of a navy. Yet it retains nearly the same organization as when it consisted only of five frigates. The rules and regulations by which it is governed earnestly call for revision, and the want of a naval school of instruction, corresponding with the Military Academy at West Point, for the formation of scientific and accomplished officers is felt with daily increasing aggravation.

The act of Congress of 26th of May, 1824, authorizing an examination and survey of the harbor of Charleston, in South Carolina, of St. Marys in Georgia and of the coast of Florida, and for other purposes has been executed so far as the appropriation would admit. Those of the 3d of March last, authorizing the establishment of a navy-yard and depot on the coast of Florida, in the Gulf of Mexico, and authorizing the building of ten sloops of war and for other purposes, are in the course of execution, for the particulars of which and other objects connected with this Department I refer to the report of the Secretary of the Navy, herewith communicated....

Upon this first occasion of addressing the Legislature of the Union, with which I have been honored, in presenting to their view the execution so far as it has been effected of the measures sanctioned by them for promoting the internal improvement of our country, I can not close the communication without recommending to their calm and persevering consideration the general principle in a more enlarged extent. The great object of the institution of civil government is the improvement of the condition of those who are parties to the social compact, and no government, in whatever form constituted, can accomplish the lawful ends of its institution but in proportion as it improves the condition of those over whom it is established. Roads and canals, by multiplying and facilitating the communications and intercourse between distant regions and multitudes of men, are among the most important means of improvement. But moral, political, intellectual improvement are duties assigned by the Author of Our Existence to social no less than to individual man. For the fulfillment of those duties governments are invested with power, and to the attainment of the end — the progressive improvement of the condition of the governed — the exercise of delegated powers is a duty as sacred and indispensable as the usurpation of powers not granted is criminal and odious. Among the first, perhaps the very first, instrument for the improvement of the condition of men is knowledge and to the acquisition of much of the knowledge adapted to the wants, the comforts, and enjoyments of human life public institutions and seminaries of learning are essential. So convinced of this was the first of my predecessors in this office, now first in the memory, as living, he was first in the hearts, of our countrymen, that once and again in his addresses to the Congresses with whom he cooperated in the public service he earnestly recommended the establishment of seminaries of learning, to prepare for all the emergencies of peace and war — a national university and a military academy. With respect to the latter, had he lived to the present day, in turning his eyes to the institution at West

Point he would have enjoyed the gratification of his most earnest wishes; but in surveying the city which has been honored with his name he would have seen the spot of earth which he had destined and bequeathed to the use and benefit of his country as the site for a university still bare and barren.

In assuming her station among the civilized nations of the earth it would seem that our country had contracted the engagement to contribute her share of mind, of labor, and of expense to the improvement of those parts of knowledge which lie beyond the reach of individual acquisition, and particularly to geographical and astronomical science. Looking back to the history only of the half century since the declaration of our independence and observing the generous emulation with which the Governments of France, Great Britain, and Russia have devoted the genius, the intelligence, the treasures of their respective nations to the common improvement of the species in these branches of science, it is incumbent upon us to inquire whether we are not bound by obligations of a high and honorable character to contribute our portion of energy and exertion to the common stock. The voyages of discovery prosecuted in the course of that time at the expense of those nations have not only rebounded to their glory, but to the improvement of human knowledge. We have been partakers of that improvement and owe for it a sacred debt, not only of gratitude, but of equal or proportional exertion in the same common cause. Of the cost of these undertakings, if the mere expenditures of outfit, equipment and completion of the expeditions were to be considered the only charges, it would be unworthy of a great and generous nation to take a second thought. One hundred expeditions of circumnavigation like those of Cook and La Perouse would not burden the exchequer of the nation fitting them out so much as the ways and means of defraying a single campaign in war. But if we take into the account the lives of those benefactors of mankind of which their services in the cause of their species were the purchase, how shall the cost of those heroic enterprises be estimated, and what compensation can be made to them or to their countries for them? Is it not by bearing them in affectionate remembrance? Is it not still more by imitating their example — by enabling countrymen of our own to pursue the same career and to hazard their lives in the same cause?

In inviting the attention of Congress to the subject of internal improvements upon a view thus enlarged it is not my design to recommend the equipment of expedition for circumnavigating the globe for purposes of scientific research and inquiry. We have objects of useful investigation nearer home, and to which our cares may be more beneficially applied. The interior of our own territories has yet been very imperfectly explored. Our coasts along many degrees of latitude upon the shores of the Pacific Ocean, though much frequented by spirited commercial navigators, have been barely visited by our public ships. The River of the West, first fully discovered and navigated by a countryman of our own, still bears the name of the ship in which he ascended its waters, and claims the protection of our armed national flag at its mouth. With the establishment of a military post there or at some other point of that coast, recommended by my predecessor and already matured in the deliverations of the last Congress, I would suggest the expediency of connecting the equipment of a public ship for the exploration of the whole northwest coast of this continent.

The establishment of an uniform standard of weights and measures was one of the specific objects contemplated in the formation of our Constitution and to fix that standard was one of the powers delegated by express terms in that instrument to Congress. The Governments of Great Britain and France have scarcely ceased to be occupied with inquiries and speculations on the same subject since the existence of our Constitution, and with them it has expanded into profound, laborious, and expensive researches into the figure of the earth and the comparative length of the pendulum vibrating seconds in various latitudes from the equator to the pole. These researches have resulted in the composition and publication of several works highly interesting to the cause of science. The experiments are yet in the process of performance. Some of them have recently been made on our own shores, within the walls of one of our own colleges, and partly by one of our own fellow-citizens. It would be honorable to our country if the sequel of the same experiments should be countenanced by the patronage of our Government, as they have been hitherto been by those of France and Britain.

Connected with the establishment of an university, or separate from it, might be undertaken the erection of an astronomical observatory, with provision for the support of an astronomer, to be in constant attendance of observation upon the phenomena of the heavens, and for the periodical publication of his observations. It is with no feeling of pride as an American that the remark may be made that on the comparatively small territorial surface of Europe there are existing upward of 130 of these light-houses of the skies, while throughout the whole American hemisphere there is not one. If we reflect a moment upon the discoveries which in the last four centuries have been made in the physical constitution of the universe by means of these building and of observers stationed in them, shall we doubt of their usefulness to every nation? And while scarcely a year passes over our heads without bringing some new astronomical discovery to light, which we must fain receive at second hand from Europe, are we not cutting ourselves off from the means of returning light for light while we have neither observatory nor observer upon our half of the globe and the earth revolves in perpetual darkness to our unsearching eyes?...

On the 24th of December, 1799, it was resolved by Congress that a marble monument should be erected by the United States in the Capitol at the city of Washington; that the family of General Washington should be requested to permit his body to be deposited under it, and that the monument be so designed as to commemorate the great events of his military and political life. In reminding Congress of this resolution and that the monument contemplated by it remains yet without execution, I shall indulge only the remarks that the works at the Capitol are approaching to completion; that the consent of the family, desired by the resolution, was requested and obtained; that a monument has been recently erected in this city over the remains of another distinguished patroit of the Revolution, and that a spot has been reserved within the walls where you are deliberating for the benefit of this and future ages, in which the mortal remains may be deposited by him whose spirit hovers over you and listens with delight to every act of the representatives of his nation which can tend to exault and adorn his and their oountry....

The spirit of improvement is abroad upon the earth. It stimulates the heart and sharpens the faculties not of our fellow-citizens alone, but of the nations of Europe and of their rulers. While dwelling with pleasing satisfaction upon the superior excellence of our political institutions, let us not be unmindful that liberty is power; that the nation blessed with the largest portion of liberty must in proportion to its numbers be the most powerful nation upon the earth.

## THE PANAMA CONGRESS MESSAGE
### December 26, 1825

*When Adams asked the Senate to confirm the envoys to the Panama Congress, the Jacksonians had their first opportunity to discredit him. They finally approved the nominations, but only after much debate and political maneuvering.*

To the Senate of the United States;

In the message to both Houses of Congress at the commencement of the session it was mentioned that the Governments of the Republics of Colombia, of Mexico, and of Central America had severally invited the Government of the United States to be represented at the Congress of American nations to be assembled at Panama to deliberate upon objects of peculiar concernment to this hemisphere, and that this invitation had been accepted.

Although this measure was deemed to be within the constitutional competency of the Executive, I have not thought proper to take any step in it before ascertaining that my opinion of its expediency will concur with that of both branches of the Legislature, first by the decision of the Senate upon the nominations to be laid before them, and secondly, by the sanction of both Houses to the appropriations, without which it can not be carried into effect.

A report from the Secretary of State and copies of the correspondence with the South American Governments on this subject since the invitation given by them are herewith transmitted to the Senate. They will disclose the objects of importance which are expected to form a subject of discussion at this meeting, in which interests of high importance to this Union are involved. It will be seen that the United States neither intend nor are expected to take part in any deliberations of a belligerent character; that the motive of their attendance is neither to contract alliances nor to engage in any undertaking or project importing hostility to any other nation.

But the Southern American nations, in the infancy of their independence, often find themselves in positions with reference to other countries with the principles applicable to which, derivable from the state of independence itself, they have not been familiarized by experience. The result of this has been that sometimes in their intercourse with the United States they have manifested dispositions to reserve a right of granting special favors and privileges to the Spanish nation as the price of their recognition. At others they have actually established duties and impositions operating unfavorably to the United States to the advantage of other European powers, and sometimes they have appeared to consider that they might interchange among themselves mutual concessions of exclusive favor, to which neither European powers nor the United States should be admitted. In most of these cases their regulations unfavorable to us have yielded to friendly expostulation and remonstrance. But it is believed to be of infinite moment that the principles of a liberal commercial intercourse should be exhibited to them, and urged with disinterested and friendly persuasion upon them when all assembled for the avowed purpose of consulting together upon the establishment of such principles as may have an important bearing upon their future welfare.

The consentaneous adoption of principles of maritime neutrality, and favorable to the navigation of peace, and commerce in time of war, will also form a subject of consideration to this Congress. The doctrine that free ships make free goods and the restriction of reason upon the extent of blockades may be established by general agreement with far more ease, and perhaps with less danger, by the general engagement to adhere to them concerted at such a meeting, than by partial treaties or conventions with each of the nations separately. An agreement between all the parties represented at the meeting that each will guard by its own means against the establishment of any future European colony within its borders may be found advisable. This was more than two years since announced by my predecessor to the world as a principle resulting from the emancipation of both the

American continents. It may be so developed to the new southern nations that they will all feel it as an essential appendage to their independence.

There is yet another subject upon which, without entering into any treaty, the moral influence of the United States may perhaps be exerted with beneficial consequences at such a meeting – the advancement of religious liberty. Some of the southern nations are even yet so far under the dominion of prejudice that they have incorporated with their political constitutions an exclusive church, without toleration of any other than the dominant sect. The abandonment of this last badge of religious bigotry and oppression may be pressed more effectually by the united exertions of those who concur in the principles of freedom of conscience upon those who are yet to be convinced of their justice and wisdom than by the solitary efforts of a minister to any one of the separate Governments.

The indirect influence which the United States may exercise upon any project or purposes originating in the war in which the southern Republics are still engaged, which might seriously affect the interest of this Union, and the good offices by which the United States may ultimately contribute to bring that war to a speedier termination, though among the motives which have convinced me of the propriety of complying with this invitation, are so far contingent and eventual that it would be improper to dwell upon them more at large.

In fine, a decisive inducement with me for acceding to the measure is to show by this token of respect to the southern Republics the interest that we take in their welfare and our disposition to comply with their wishes. Having been the first to recognize their independence, and sympathized with them so far as was compatible with our neutral duties in all their struggles and sufferings to acquire it, we have laid the foundation of our future intercourse with them in the broadest principles of reciprocity and the most cordial feelings of fraternal friendship. To extend those principles to all our commercial relations with them and to hand down that friendship to future ages is congenial to the highest policy of the Union, as it will be that of all those nations and their posterity. In the confidence that these sentiments will meet the approbation of the Senate, I nominate Richard C. Anderson, of Kentucky and John Sergeant, of Pennsylvania, to be envoys extraordinary and ministers plenipotentiary to the assembly of American nations at Panama, and William B. Rochester of New York, to be secretary to the mission.

## SECOND ANNUAL MESSAGE
### December 5, 1826

*The key element in the second address is the report on
the American-British trade problems. Adams would receive
no help from the Congress in trying to solve these differences, and his inability to recapture the West Indian
Trade played an important part in his losing the election
of 1828.*

Fellow-Citizens of the Senate and of the House of Representatives:

The assemblage of the representatives of our Union in both Houses
of the Congress at this time occurs under circumstances calling for
the renewed homage of our grateful acknowledgments to the Giver of
All Good. With the exceptions incidental to the most felicitous condition of human existence, we continue to be highly favored in all the
elements which contribute to individual comfort and to national prosperity. In the survey of our extensive country we have generally to
observe abodes of health and regions of plenty. In our civil and political
relations we have peace without and tranquillity within our borders.
We are, as a people, increasing with unabated rapidity in population,
wealth, and national resources, and whatever differences of opinion
exist among us with regard to the mode and the means by which we
shall turn the beneficence of Heaven to the improvement of our own
condition, there is yet a spirit animating us all which will not suffer
the bounties of Providence to be showered upon us in vain, but will
receive them with grateful hearts, and apply them with unwearied
hands to the advancement of the general good.

Of the subjects recommended to Congress at their last session,
some were then definitively acted upon. Others, left unfinished, but
partly matured, will recur to your attention without needing a renewal
of notice from me. The purpose of this communication will be to present to your view the general aspect of our public affairs at this moment and the measures which have been taken to carry into effect the
intentions of the Legislature as signified by the laws then and heretofore enacted.

In our intercourse with the other nations of the earth we have still
the happiness of enjoying peace and a general good understanding, qualified, however, in several important instances by collisions of interest
and by unsatisfied claims of justice, to the settlement of which the
constitutional interposition of the legislative authority may become
ultimately indispensable.

By the decease of the Emperor Alexander of Russia, which occurred cotemporaneously with the commencement of the last session
of Congress, the United States have been deprived of a long-tried,
steady, and faithful friend. Born to the inheritance of absolute power
and trained in the school of adversity, from which no power on earth,
however absolute, is exempt, that monarch from his youth had been

taught to feel the force and value of public opinion and to be sensible that the interests of his own Government would best be promoted by a frank and friendly inter-liberal commercial intercourse with our country. A candid and confidential interchange of sentiments between him and the Government of the United States upon the affairs of Southern America took place at a period not long preceding his demise, and contributed to fix that course of policy which left to the other Governments of Europe no alternative but that of sooner or later recognizing the independence of our southern neighbors, of which the example had by the United States already been set. The ordinary diplomatic communications between his successor, the Emperor Nicholas, and the United States have suffered some interruption by the illness, departure, and subsequent decease of his minister residing here, who enjoyed, as he merited, the entire confidence of his new sovereign, as he had eminently responded to that of his predecessor. But we have had the most satisfactory assurances that the sentiments of the reigning Emperor toward the United States are altogether conformable to those which had so long and constantly animated his imperial brother, and we have reason to hope that they will serve to cement that harmony and good understanding between the two nations which, founded in congenial interests, can not but result in the advancement of the welfare and prosperity of both.

Our relations of commerce and navigation with France are, by the operation of the convention of 24th of June, 1822, with that nation, in a state of gradual and progressive improvement. Convinced by all our experience, no less than by the principles of fair and liberal reciprocity which the United States have constantly tendered to all the nations of the earth as the rule of commercial intercourse which they would universally prefer, that fair and equal competition is most conducive to the interests of both parties, the United States in the negotiation of that convention earnestly contended for a mutual renunciation of discriminating duties and charges in the ports of the two countries. Unable to obtain the immediate recognition of this principle in its full extent, after reducing the duties of discrimination so far as was found attainable, it was agreed that at the expiration of two years from the 1st of October, 1822, when the convention was to go into effect, unless a notice of six months on either side should be given to the other that the convention itself must terminate, those duties should be reduced one-fourth, and that this reduction should be yearly repeated, until all discrimination should cease, while the convention itself should continue in force. By the effect of this stipulation three-fourths of the discriminating duties which had been levied by each party upon the vessels of the other in its ports have already been removed; and on the 1st of next October, should the convention be still in force, the remaining fourth will be discontinued. French vessels laden with French produce will be received in our ports on the same terms as our own, and ours in return will enjoy the same advantages in the ports of France....

With the Government of the Netherlands the mutual abandonment of discriminating duties had been regulated by legislative acts on both sides. The act of Congress of the 20th April, 1818, abolished all discriminating duties of impost and tonnage upon the vessels and produce of the Netherlands in the ports of the United States upon the assurance given by the Government of the Netherlands that all such duties operating against the shipping and commerce of the United States in that Kingdom had been abolished. These reciprocal regulations had continued in force several years when the discriminating principle was resumed by the Netherlands in a new and indirect form by a bounty of 10 per cent in the shape of a return of duties to their national vessels, and in which those of the United States are not permitted to participate. By the act of Congress of 7th January, 1824, all discriminating duties in the United States were again suspended, so far as related to the vessels and produce of the Netherlands, so long as the reciprocal exemption should be extended to the vessels and produce of the United States in the Netherlands. But the same act provides that in the event of a restoration of discriminating duties to operate against the shipping and commerce of the United States in any of the foreign countries referred to therein the suspension of discriminating duties in favor of the navigation of such foreign country should cease and all the provisions of the acts imposing discriminating foreign tonnage and impost duties in the United States should revive and be in full force with regard to that nation. . . .

During the last session of Congress treaties of amity, navigation, and commerce were negotiated and signed at this place with the Government of Denmark, in Europe, and with the Federation of Central America in this hemisphere. These treaties then received the constitutional sanction of the Senate, by the advice and consent to their ratification. They were accordingly ratified on the part of the United States, and during the recess of Congress have been also ratified by the other respective contracting parties. The ratifications have been exchanged, and they have been published by proclamations, copies of which are herewith communicated to Congress. . . .

In the course of the last summer the term to which our last commercial treaty with Sweden was limited has expired. A continuation of it is in the contemplation of the Swedish Government and is believed to be desirable on the part of the United States. It has been proposed by the King of Sweden that pending the negotiation of renewal the expired treaty should be mutually considered as still in force a measure which will require the sanction of Congress to be carried into effect on our part, and which I therefore recommend to your consideration. . . .

But with regard to the commercial intercourse between the United States and the British colonies in America, it has been hitherto found impracticable to bring the parties to an understanding satisfactory to both. The relative geographical position and the respective products of nature cultivated by human industry had constituted the elements of a commercial intercourse between the United States and British America, insular and continental, important to the inhabitants of both countries; but it had been interdicted by Great Britain upon a principle hereto fore practiced upon by the colonizing nations of Europe, of holding the trade of their colonies each in exclusive monopoly to herself. After the termination of the late war this interdiction had been revived, and the British Government declined including this portion of our intercourse with her possessions in the negotiation of the convention of 1815. The trade was then carried on exclusively in British vessels till the act of Congress, concerning navigation, of 1818 and the supplemental act of 1820 met the interdict by a corresponding measure on the part of the United States. These measures, not of retaliation, but of necessary self-defense, were soon succeeded by an act of Parliament opening certain colonial ports to the vessels of the United States coming directly from them, and to the importation from them of certain articles of our produce burdened with heavy duties, and excluding some of the most valuable articles of our exports. The United States opened their ports to British vessels from the colonies upon terms as exactly corresponding with those of the act of Parliament as in the relative position of the parties could be made, and a negotiation was commenced by mutual consent, with the hope on our part that a reciprocal spirit of accommodation and a common sentiment of the importance of the trade to the interests of the inhabitants of the two countries between whom it must be carried on would ultimately bring the parties to compromise with which both might be satisifed. With this view the Government of the United States had determined to sacrifice something of that entire reciprocity which in all commercial arrangements with foreign powers they are entitled to demand, and to acquiesce in some inequalities disadvantageous to ourselves rather than to forego the benefit of a final and permanent adjustment of this interest to the satisfaction of Great Britain herself. The negotiation, repeatedly suspended by accidental circumstances, was, however, by mutual agreement and express assent, considered as pending and to be speedily resumed. In the meantime another act of Parliament, so doubtful and ambiguous in its import as to have been misunderstood by the officers in the colonies who were to carry it into execution, opens again certain colonial ports upon new conditions and terms, with a threat to close them against any nation which may not accept those terms as prescribed by the British Government. This act, passed in July, 1825, not communicated to the Government of the United States, not understood by the British officers of the customs in the colonies where it was to be enforced, was nevertheless submitted to the consideration of Congress at their last session. With the knowledge that a negotiation upon the subject had long been in progress and pledges given of its resumption at an early day, it was deemed expedient to await the result of that negotiation rather than to subscribe implicitly to terms the import of which was not clear and which the British authorities themselves in this hemisphere were not prepared to explain.

immediately after the close of the last session of Congress one of our most distinguished citizens was dispatched as envoy extraordinary and minister plenipotentiary to Great Britain, furnished with instructions which we could not doubt would lead to a conclusion of this long-controverted interest upon terms acceptable to Great Britain. Upon his arrival, and before he had delivered his letters of credence, he was met by an order of the British council excluding from and after the 1st of December now current the vessels of the United States from all the colonial British ports excepting those immediately bordering on our territories. In answer to his expostulations upon a measure thus unexpected he is informed that according to the ancient maxims of policy of European nations having colonies their trade is an exclusive possession of the mother country; that all participation in it by other nations is a boon or favor not forming a subject of negotiation, but to be regulated by the legislative acts of the power owning the colony; that the British Government therefore declines negotiations concerning it, and that as the United States did not forthwith accept purely and simply the terms offered by the act of Parliament of July, 1825, Great Britain would not now admit the vessels of the United States even upon the terms on which she has opened them to the navigation of other nations.

We have been accustomed to consider the trade which we have enjoyed with the British colonies rather as an interchange of mutual benefits than as a mere favor received; that under every circumstance we have given an ample equivalent. We have seen every other nation holding colonies negotiate with other nations and grant them freely admission to the colonies by treaty, and so far are the other colonizing nations of Europe now from refusing to negotiate for trade with their colonies that we ourselves have secured access to the colonies of more than one of them by treaty. The refusal, however, of Great Britain to negotiate leaves to the United States no other alternative than that of regulating or interdicting altogether the trade on their part, according as either measure may affect the interests of our own country, and with that exclusive object I would recommend the whole subject to your calm and candid deliberations.

It is hoped that our unavailing exertions to accomplish a cordial good understanding on this interest will not have an unpropitious effect upon the other great topics of discussion between the two Governments. Our northeastern and northwestern boundaries are still unadjusted. The commissioners under the seventh article of the treaty of Ghent have nearly come to the close of their labors; nor can we renounce the expectation, enfeebled as it is that they may agree upon their report to the satisfaction or acquiescence of both parties. The commission for liquidating the claims for indemnity for slaves carried away after the close of the war has been sitting, with doubtful prospects of success. Propositions of compromise have, however, passed between the two Governments, the result of which we flatter ourselves may yet prove satisfactory. Our own dispositions and purposes toward Great Britain are all friendly and conciliatory; nor can we abandon but with strong reluctance the belief that they will ultimately meet a return not of favors, which we neither ask nor desire, but of equal reciprocity and good will. . . .

The congress of ministers from several of those nations which assembled at Panama, after a short session there, adjourned to meet again at a more favorable season in the neighborhood of Mexico. The decease of one of our ministers on his way to the Isthmus, and the impediments of the season, which delayed the departure of the other, deprived us of the advantage of being represented at the first meeting of the congress. There is, however, no reason to believe that any of the transactions of the congress were of a nature to affect injuriously the interests of the United States or to require the interposition of our ministers had they been present. Their absence has, indeed, deprived us of the opportunity of possessing precise and authentic information of the treaties which were concluded at Panama; and the whole result has confirmed me in the conviction of the expediency to the United States of being represented at the congress. The surviving member of the mission, appointed during your last session, has accordingly proceeded to his destination, and a successor to his distinguished and lamented associate will be nominated to the Senate. A treaty of amity, navigation, and commerce has in the course of the last summer been concluded by our minister plenipotentiary at Mexico with the united states of that Confederacy, which will also be laid before the Senate for their advice with regard to its ratification.

In adverting to the present condition of our fiscal concerns and to the prospects of our revenue the first remark that calls our attention is that they are less exuberantly prosperous than they were at the corresponding period of the last year. The sever shock so extensively sustained by the commercial and manufacturing interests in Great Britain has not been without a perceptible recoil upon ourselves. A reduced importation from abroad is necessarily succeeded by a reduced return to the Treasury at home. The net revenue of the present year will not equal that of the last, and the receipts of that which is to come will fall short of those in the current year. The diminution, however, is in part attributable to the flourishing condition of some of our domestic manufactures, and so far is compensated by an equivalent more profitable to the nation. It is also highly gratifying to perceive that the deficiency in the revenue, while it scarcely exceeds the anticipations of the last year's estimate from the Treasury, has not interrupted the application of more than eleven millions during the present year to the discharge of the principal and interest of the debt, nor the reduction of upward of seven millions of the capital of the debt itself. The balance in the Treasury on the 1st of January last was $5,201,650.33; the receipts from that time to the 30th of September last were $19,585,932.50; the receipts of the current quarter, estimated at $6,000,000, yield with the sums already received, a revenue of about twenty-five millions and a half for the year; the expenditures for the three first quarters of the year have amounted to $18,714,226.66; the expenditures of the current quarter are expected, including the two millions of the principal of the debt to be paid, to balance the receipts so that the expenses of the year, amounting to upward of a million less than its income, will leave a proportionally increased balance in the Treasury on the 1st of January, 1827, over that of the 1st of January last; instead of $5,200,000 there will be $6,400,000....

From the reports herewith communicated of the Secretaries of War and of the Navy, with the subsidiary documents annexed to them, will be discovered the present condition and administration of our military establishment on the land and on the sea. The organization of the Army having undergone, no change since its reduction to the present peace establishment in 1821, it remains only to observe that it is yet found adequate to all the purposes for which a permanent armed force in time of peace can be needed or useful. It may be proper to add that, from a difference of opinion between the late President of the United States and the Senate with regard to the construction of the act of Congress of 2d March, 1821, to reduce and fix the military peace establishment of the United States, it remains hitherto so far without execution that no colonel has been appointed to command one of the regiments of artillery. A supplementary or explanatory act of the Legislature appears to be the only expedient practicable for removing the difficulty of this appointment.

In a period of profound peace the conduct of the mere military establishment form but a very inconsiderable portion of the duties devolving upon the administration of the Department of War....

By the act of the 30th of April 1824, suggested and approved by my predecessor, the sum of $30,000 was appropriated for the purpose of causing to be made the necessary surveys, plans and estimates of the routes of such roads and canals as the President of the United States might deem of national importance in a commercial or military point of view, or necessary for the transportation of the public mail. The surveys, plans, and estimates for each, when completed, will be laid before Congress.

In execution of this act a board of engineers was immediately instituted and have been since most assiduously and constantly occupied in carrying it into effect. The first object to which their labors were directed, by order of the late President, was the examination of the country between the tide waters of the Potomac, the Ohio, and Lake Erie, to ascertain the practicability of a communication between them, to designate the most suitable route for the same, and to form plans and estimates in detail for the expense of execution.

On the 3d of February, 1825, they made their first report, which was immediately communicated to Congress, and in which they declared that having maturely considered the circumstances observed by them personally, and carefully studied the results of such of the preliminary surveys as were then completed, they were decidedly of opinion that the communication was practicable.

At the last session of Congress, before the board of engineers were enabled to make up their second report containing a general plan and preparatory estimate for the work the Committee of the House of Representatives upon Roads and Canals closed the session with a report expressing the hope that the plan and estimate of the board of engineers might at this time be prepared, and that the subject be referred to the early and favorable consideration of Congress at their present session. That expected report of the board of engineers is prepared and will forthwith be laid before you. . . .

Of the small portions of this Navy engaged in actual service during the peace, squadrons have continued to be maintained in the Pacific Ocean, in the West India seas, and in the Mediterranean, to which has been added a small armament to cruise on the eastern coast of South America. In all they have afforded protection to our commerce, have contributed to make our country advantageously known to foreign nations, have honorably employed multitudes of our seamen in the service of their country, and have inured numbers of youths of the rising generation to lives of manly hardihood and of nautical experience and skill. The piracies with which the West India seas were for several years infested have been totally supressed, but in the Mediterranean they have increased in a manner afflictive to other nations, and but for the continued presence of our squadron would probably have been distressing to our own. The war which has unfortunately broken out between the Republic of Buenos Ayres and the Brazilian Government has given rise to very great irregularities among the naval officers of the latter by whom principles in relation to blockades and to neutral navigation have been brought forward to which we can not subscribe and which our own commanders have found it necessary to resist. From the friendly disposition toward the United States constantly manifested by the Emperor of Brazil, and the very useful and friendly commercial intercourse between the United States and his dominions, we have reason to believe that the just reparation demanded for the injuries sustained by several of our citizens from some of his officers will not be withheld. Abstracts from the recent dispatches of the commanders of our several squadrons are communicated with the report of the Secretary of the Navy to Congress.

A report from the Postmaster-General is likewise communicated, presenting in a highly satisfactory manner the result of a vigorous,

efficient and economical administration of that Department. The
revenue of the office, even of the year including the latter half of 1824
and the first half of 1825, had exceeded its expenditures by a sum of
more than $45,000. That of the succeeding year has been still more
productive. The increase of the receipts in the year preceding the 1st
of July last over that of the year before exceeds $136,000, and the
excess of the receipts over the expenditures of the year has swollen
from $45,000 to nearly $80,000. During the same period contracts
for additional transportation of the mail in stages for about 260,000
miles have been made and for 70,000 miles annually on horseback.
Seven hundred and fourteen new postoffices have been established
within the year, and the increase of revenue within the last three
years, as well as the augmentation of the transportation by mail, is
more than equal to the whole amount of receipts and of mail convey-
ance at the commencement of the present century, when the seat of
the General Government was removed to this place. When we reflect
that the objects effected by the transportation of the mail are among
the choicest comforts and enjoyments of social life, it is pleasing to
observe that the dissemination of them to every corner of our country
has outstripped in their increase even the rapid march of our population.

By the treaties with France and Spain, respectively ceding
Louisiana and the Floridas to the United States, provision was made
for the security of land titles derived from the Governments of those
nations. Some progress has been made under the authority of various
acts of Congress in the ascertainment and establishment of those
titles, but claims to a very large extent remain unadjusted. The public
faith no less than the just rights of individuals and the interest of
the community itself appears to require further provisions for the
speedy settlement of these claims, which I therefore recommend to
the care and attention of the Legislature.

In conformity with the provisions of the act of 20th May last, to
provide for erecting a penitentiary in the District of Columbia, and
for other purposes, three commissioners were appointed to select a
site for the erection of a penitentiary for the District, and also a site
in the county of Alexandria for a county jail, both of which objects
have been effected. The building of the penitentiary has been commenced, and is in such a degree of forwardness as to promise that it
will be completed before the meeting of the next Congress. This consideration points to the expediency of maturing at the present session a system for the regulation and government of the penitentiary,
and of defining the class of offenses which shall be punishable by
confinement in this edifice.

In closing this communication I trust that it will not be deemed
inappropriate to the occasion and purposes upon which we are here
assembled to indulge a momentary retrospect, combining in a single

glance the period of our origin as a national confederation with that of our present existence, at the precise interval of half a century from each other. Since your last meeting at this place the fiftieth anniversary of the day when our independence was declared has been celebrated throughout our land, and on that day, while every heart was bounding with joy and every voice was tuned to gratualation, amid the blessings of freedom and independence which the sires of a former age had handled down to their children, two of the principal actors in that solemn scene — the hand that penned the ever-memorable Declaration and the voice that sustained it in debate — were by one summons, at the distance of 700 miles from each other called before the Judge of All to account for their deeds done upon earth. They departed cheered by the benedictions of their country to whom they left the inheritance of their fame and memory of their bright example. If we turn our thoughts to the condition of their country, in contrast of the first and last day of that half century, how resplendent and sublime is the transition from gloom to glory. . . .

## THIRD ANNUAL MESSAGE
### December 4, 1827

*The message was more important for what it didn't contain than for what it did. By not mentioning a protective tariff, Adams offended most of the few supporters he had left in Congress.*

Fellow-Citizens of the Senate and of the House of Representatives:

A revolution of the seasons has nearly been completed since the representatives of the people and States of this Union were last assembled at this place to deliverate and to act upon the common important interests of their constituents . . . .

Our relations of friendship with the other nations of the earth, political and commercial, have been preserved unimpaired, and the opportunities to improve them have been cultivated with anxious and unremitting attention. A negotiation upon subjects of high and delicate interest with the Government of Great Britain has terminated in the adjustment of some of the questions at issue upon satisfactory terms and the postponement of others for future discussion and agreement. The purposes of the convention concluded at St. Petersburg on the 12th day of July, 1822, under the mediation of the late Emperor Alexander, have been carried into effect by a subsequent convention, concluded at London on the 13th of November, 1826, the ratifications of which were exchanged at that place on the 6th day of February last. A copy of the proclamation issued on the 19th day of March last, publishing this convention, is herewith communicated to Congress. The sum of $1,204,960, therein stipulated to be paid to the claimants of indemnity under the first article of the treaty of Ghent, has been duly received, and the commission instituted comformably to the act of Congress of the 2d of March last, for the distribution of the indemnity to the persons entitled to receive it are now in session and approaching the consummation of their labors....

The conventions of 3d July, 1815, and of 20th October, 1818 will expire by their own limitation on the 20th of October 1828. These have regulated the direct commercial intercourse between the United States and Great Britain upon terms of the most perfect reciprocity; and they effected a temporary compromise of the respective rights and claims to territory westward of the Rocky Mountains. These arrangements have been continued for an indefinite period of time after the expiration of the above-mentioned conventions, leaving each party the liberty of terminating them by giving twelve months notice to the other. The radical principle of all commercial intercourse between independent nations is the mutual interest of both parties. It is the vital spirit of trade itself; nor can it be reconciled to the nature of man or to the primary laws of human society that any traffic should long be willingly pursued of which all the advantages are on one side and all the burdens on the other. Treaties of commerce have been found by experience to be among the most effective instruments for promoting peace and harmony between nations whose interests, exclusively considered on either side, are brought into frequent collision by compeition. In framing such treaties it is the duty of each party not simply to urge with unyielding pertinacity that which suits its own interest, but to concede liberally to that which is adapted to the interest of the other. To accomplish this, little more is generally required than a simple observance of the rule of reciprocity, and were it possible for the statesmen of one nation by stratagem and management to obtain from the weakness or ignorance of another an over-reaching treaty, such a compact would prove an incentive to war rather than a bond of peace. Our conventions with Great Britain are founded upon the principles of reciprocity. The commercial intercourse between the two countries is greater in magnitude and amount than between any two other nations on the globe. It is for all purposes of benefit or advantage to both as precdous and in all probability far more extensive, than if the parties were still constituent parts of one and the same nation. Treaties between such states, regulating the intercourse of peace between them and adjusting interests of such transcendent importance to both, which have been found in a long experience of years mutually advantageous, should not be lightly canceled or discontinued. Two conventions for countinuing in force those above mentioned have been concluded between the plenipotentiaries of the two Governments on the 6th of August last, and will be forthwith laid before the Senate for the exercise of their constitutional authority concerning them.

In the execution of the treaties of peace of November 1782, and September, 1783, between the United States and Great Britain, and which terminated the war of our independence, a line of boundary was drawn as the demarcation of territory between the two countries, extending over near 20 degrees of latitude and ranging over seas, lakes, and mountains.... In the progress of discovery and settlement of both parties since that time several questions of boundary between their respective territories have arisen, which have been found of exceedingly difficult adjustment. At the close of the last war with Great Britain four of these questions pressed themselves upon the consideration of the negotiators of the treaty of Ghent, but without the means of concluding a definitive arrangement concerning them. They were referred to three separate commissions consisting of two commissioners, one appointed by each party, to examine and decide upon their respective claims. In the event of a disagreement between the commissioners it was provided that they should make reports to their several Governments, and that the reports should finally be referred to the decision of a sovereign the common friend of both. Of these commissioners two have already terminated their sessions and investigations, one by entire and the other by partial agreement. The commissioners of the fifth article of the treaty of Ghent have finally disagreed, and made their conflicting reports to their own Governments. But from these reports a great difficulty has occurred in making up a question to be decided by the arbitrator. The purpose has, however, been effected by a fourth convention, concluded at London by the pleinpotentiaries of the two Governments on the 29th of September last. It will be submitted, together with the others, to the consideration of the Senate.

While these questions have been pending incidents have occurred of conflicting pretensions and of dangerous character upon the territory itself in dispute between the two nations. By a common understanding between the Governments it was agreed that no exercise of exclusive jurisdiction by either party while the negotiation was pending should change the state of the question of right to be definitively settled. Such collision has, nevertheless, recently taken place by occurrences the precise character of which has not yet been ascertained. A communication from the governor of the State of Maine, with accompanying documents, and a correspondence between the Secretary of State and the minister of Great Britain on this subject are now communicated. Measures have been taken to ascertain the state of the facts more corectly by the employment of a special agent to visit the spot where the alleged outrages have occurred, the result of whose inquiries, when received, will be transmitted to Congress.

While so many of the subjects of high interest to the friendly relations between the two countries have been so far adjusted, it is a matter of regret that their views respecting the commercial intercourse

between the United States and the British colonial possessions have
not equally approximated to a friendly agreement.

At the commencement of the last session of Congress they were
informed of the sudden and unexpected exclusion by the British Government of access in vessels of the United States to all their colonial ports
except those immediately bordering upon our own territories. In the
amicable discussions which have succeeded the adoption of this measure, which, as it affected harshly the interests of the United States,
became a subject of expostulation on our part, the principles upon
which its justification has been placed have been of a diversified
character. It has been at once ascribed to a mere recurrence to the
old, long-established principle of colonial monopoly and at the same
time to a feeling of resentment because the offers of an act of Parliament opening the colonial ports upon certain conditions had not been
grasped at with sufficient eagerness by an instantaneous conformity
to them. At a subsequent period it has been intimated that the new
exclusion was in resentment because a prior act of Parliment of 1822,
opening certain colonial ports, under heavy and burdensome restrictions, to vessels of the United States, had not been reciprocated by an
admission of British vessels from the colonies and their cargoes,
without any restriction or discrimination whatever. But be the motive
for the interdiction what it may, the British Government have manifested no dispostion, either by negotiation or by corresponding legislative enactments, to recede from it, and we have been given distinct-
ly to understand that neither of the bills which were under the consideration of Congress at their last session would have been deemed
sufficient in their concessions to have been rewarded by any relaxation
from the British interdict. It is one of the inconveniences inseparably
connected with the attempt to adjust by reciprocal legislation interests
of this nature that neither party can know what would be satisfactory
to the other, and that after enacting a statute for the avowed and sin-
cere purpose of conciliation it will generally be found utterly inadequate to the expectations of the other party, and will terminate in
mutual disappointment.

The session of Congress having terminated without any act upon
the subject, a proclamation was issued on the 17th of March last, conformably to the provisions of the sixth section of the act of 1st March,
1823, declaring the fact that the trade and intercourse authorized by
the British act of Parliament of 24th June, 1822, between the United
States and the British enumerated colonial ports had been by the subsequent acts of Parliament of 5th July, 1825, and the order of council
of 27th July, 1826, prohibited. The effect of this proclamation by the
terms of the act under which it was issued, has been that each and
every provision of the act concerning navigation of 18th April 1818,
and of the act supplementary thereto of 15th May, 1820, revived and
is in full force. Such, then, is the present condition of the trade that,
useful as it is to both parties, it can, with a single momentary ex-

ception, be carried on directly by the vessels of neither. That exception itself is found in a proclamation of the governor of the islands of St. Christopher and of the Virgin Islands, inviting for three months from the 28th of August last the importation of the articles of the produce of the United States which constitute their export portion of this trade in the vessels of all nations. That period having already expired, the state of mutual interdiction has again taken place. The British Government have not only declined negotiation upon this subject, but by the principle they have assumed with reference to it have precluded even the means of negotiation. It becomes not the self respect of the United States either to solicit gratuitous favors or to accept as the grant of a favor that for which an ample equivalent is exacted. It remains to be determined by the respective Governments whether the trade shall be opened by acts of reciprocal legislation. It is, in the meantime, satisfactory to know that apart from the inconveniences resulting from a disturbance of the usual channels of trade no loss has been sustained by the commerce, the navigation, or the revenue of the United States, and none of magnitude is to be apprehended from this existing state of mutual interdict.

With the other maritime and commercial nations of Europe our intercourse continues with little variation. Since the cessation by the convention of June, 1822, of all discriminating duties upon the vessels of the United States and of France in either country our trade with that nation has increased and is increasing. A disposition on the part of France has been manifested to renew that negotiation, and in acceding to the proposal we have expressed the wish that it might be extended to other subjects upon which a good understanding between the parties would be beneficial to the interests of both. The origin of the political relations between the United States and France is coeval with the first years of our independence. The memory of it is interwoven with that of our arduous struggle for national existence. Weakened as it has occasionally been since that time, it can by us never be forgotten, and we should hail with exultation the moment which should indicate a recollection equally friendly in spirit on the part of France. A fresh effort has recently been made by the minister of the United States residing at Paris to obtain a consideration of the just claims of citizens of the United States to the reparation of wrongs long since committed, many of them frankly acknowledged and all of them entitled upon every principle of justice to a candid examination. The proposal last made to the French Government has been to refer the subject which has formed an obstacle to this consideration to the determination of a sovereign the common friend of both. To this offer no definitive answer has been received, but the gallant and honorable spirit which has at all times been the pride and glory of France will not ultimately permit the demands of innocent sufferers to be extinguished in the mere consciousness of the power to reject them.

A new treaty of amity, navigation, and commerce has been concluded with the Kingdom of Sweden, which will be submitted to the
Senate for their advice with regard to its ratification. At a more recent date a minister plenipotentiary from the Hanseatic Republics
of Hamburg, Lubeck, and Bremen has been received, charged with a
special mission for the negotiation of a treaty of amity and commerce
between that ancient and renowned league and the United States. This
negotiation has accordingly been commenced, and is now in progress,
the result of which will, if successful, be also submitted to the Senate
for their consideration.

Since the accession of the Emperor Nicholas to the imperial throne
of all the Russias the friendly dispositions toward the United States
so constantly manifested by his predecessor have continued unabated,
and have been recently testified by the appointment of a minister
pleinipotentiary to reside at this place. From the interest taken by
this Sovereign in behalf of the suffering Greeks and from the spirit
with which others of the great European powers are cooperating with
him the friends of freedom and of humanity may indulge the hope that
they will obtain relief from that most unequal of conflicts which they
have so long and so gallantly sustained; they will enjoy the blessing
of self-government which by their sufferings in the cause of liberty
they have richly earned, and that their independence will be secured
by those liberal institutions of which their country furnished the
earliest examples in the history of mankind and which have conse-
crated to immortal remembrance the very soil for which they are now
again profusely pouring forth their blood. The sympathies which the
people and Government of the United States have so warmly indulged
with their cause have been acknowledged by their Government in a
letter of thanks, which I have received from their illustrious President, a translation of which is now communicated to Congress, the
representatives of that nation to whom this tribute of gratitude was
intended to be paid and to whom it was justly due.

In the American hemisphere the cause of freedom and independence
has continued to prevail, and if signalized by none of those splendid
triumphs which had crowned with glory some of the preceding years
it has only been from the banishment of all external force against
which the struggle had been maintained. The shout of victory has been
superseded by the expulsion of the enemy over whom it could have
been achieved. Our friendly wishes and cordial good will, which have
constantly followed the southern nations of America in all the vicissitudes of their war of independence, are succeeded by a solicitude
equally ardent and cordial that by the wisdom and purity of their institutions they may secure to themselves the choicest blessings of
social order and the best rewards of virtuous liberty. Disclaiming
alike all right and all intentions of interfering in those concerns
which it is the prerogative of their independence to regulate as to
them shall seem fit, we hail with joy every indication of their pros-

perity, of their harmony, of their persevering and inflexible homage to those principles of freedom and of equal rights which are alone suited to the genius and temper of the American nations. It has been, therefore, with some concern that we have observed indications of intestine divisions in some of the Republics of the south, and appearances of less union with one another than we believe to be the interest of all. Among the results of this state of things has been that the treaties concluded at Panama do not appear to have been ratified by the contracting parties, and that the meeting of the congress at Tacubaya has been indefinitely postponed. In accepting the invitations to be represented at this congress, while a manifestation was intended on the part of the United States of the most friendly disposition toward the southern Republics by whom it had been proposed, it was hoped that it would furnish an opportunity for bringing all the nations of this hemisphere to the common acknowledgment and adoption of the principles in the regulation of their internal relations which would have secured a lasting peace and harmony between them and have promoted the cause of mutual benevolence throughout the globe. But as obstacles appear to have arisen to the reassembling of the congress, one of the two ministers commissioned on the part of the United States has returned to the bosom of his country, while the minister charged with the ordinary mission to Mexico remains authorized to attend at the conferences of the congress whenever they may be resumed.

A hope was for a short time entertained that a treaty of peace actually signed between the Governments of Buenos Ayres and of Brazil would supersede all further occasion for those collisions between belligerent pretensions and neutral rights which are so commonly the result of the relations between the United States and the Brazilian Governments. At their last session Congress were informed that some of the naval officers of that Empire had advanced and practiced upon principles in relation to blockades and to neutral navigation which we could not sanction, and which our commanders found it necessary to resist. It appears that they have not been sustained by the Government of Brazil itself. Some of the vessels captured under the assumed authority of these erroneous principles have been restored, and we trust that our just expectations will be realized that adequate indemnity will be made to all the citizens of the United States who have suffered by the unwarranted captures which the Brazilian tribunals themselves have pronounced unlawful. . . .

During the last summer a detachment of the Army has been usefully and successfully called to perform their appropriate duties. At the moment when the commissioners appointed for carrying into execution certain provisions of the treaty of August 19, 1825, with various tribes of the Northwestern Indians were about to arrive at the appointed place of meeting the unprovoked murder of several citizens and other acts of unequivocal hostility committed by a party of the

Winnebago tribe, one of those associated in the treaty, followed by indications of a menacing character among other tribes of the same region, rendered necessary and immediate display of the defensive and protective force of the Union in that quarter. It was accordingly exhibited by the immediate and concerted movements of the governors of the State of Illinois and of the Territory of Michigan, and competent levies of militia, under their authority, with a corps of 700 men of United States troops, under the command of General Atkinson, who, at the call of Governor Cass, immediately repaired to the scene of danger from their station in St. Louis. Their presence dispelled the alarms of our fellow-citizens on those borders, and overawed the hostile purposes of the Indians. The perpetrators of the murders were surrendered to the authority and operation of our laws, and every appearance of purposed hostility from those Indian tribes has subsided. . . .

The expediency of providing for additional numbers of officers in the two corps of engineers will in some degree depend upon the number and extent of the objects of national importance upon which Congress may think it proper that surveys should be made conformably to the act of the 30th of April, 1824. Of the surveys which before the last session of Congress had been made under the authority of that act, reports were made —

1. Of the Board of Internal Improvement, on the Chesapeake and Ohio Canal.

2. On the continuation of the national road from Cumberland to the tide waters within the District of Columbia.

3. On the continuation of the national road from Canton to Zanesville.

4. On the location of the national road from Zanesville to Columbus.

5. On the continuation of the same to the seat of government in Missouri.

6. On a post-road from Baltimore to Philadelphia.

7. Of a survey of Kennebec River (in part).

8. On a national road from Washington to Buffalo.

9. On the survey of Saugatuck Harbor and River.

10. On a canal from Lake Pontchartrain to the Mississippi River.

11. On surveys at Edgartown, Newburyport, and Hyannis Harbor.

12. On survey of La Plaisance Bay, in the Territory of Michigan.

And reports are now prepared and will be submitted to Congress—

On surveys of the peninsula of Florida, to ascertain the practicability of a canal to connect the waters of the Atlantic with the Gulf of Mexico across that peninsula, with the view of connecting them together by a canal.

On surveys of a route for a canal to connect the waters of James and Great Kenhawa rivers.

On the survey of the Swash, in Pamlico Sound, and that of Cape Fear, below the town of Wilmington in North Carolina.

On the survey of the Muscle Shoals in the Tennessee River, and for a route for a contemplated communication between the Hiwassee and Coosa rivers, in the State of Alabama.

Other reports of surveys upon objects pointed out by the several acts of Congress of the last and preceding sessions are in the progress of preparation, and most of them may be completed before the close of this session. All the officers of both corps of engineers, with several other persons duly qualified, have been constantly employed upon these services from the passage of the act of 30th April, 1824, to this time. Were no other advantage to accrue to the country from their labors than the fund of topographical knowledge which they have collected and communicated, that alone would have been a profit to the Union more than adequate to all the expenditures which have been devoted to the object; but the appropriations for the repair and continuation of the Cumberland road, for the construction of various other roads, for the removal of obstructions from the rivers and harbors, for the erection of light-houses, beacons, piers, and buoys, and for the completion of canals undertaken by individual associations, but needing the assistance of means and resources more comprehensive than individual enterprise can command, may be considered rather as treasure laid up from the contributions of the present age for the benefit of posterity than as unrequited applications of the accruing revenues of the nation. To such objects of permanent improvement to the condition of the country, of real addition to the wealth as well as to the comfort of the people by whose authority and resources they have been effected, from three to four millions of the annual income of the nation have, by laws enacted at the three most recent sessions of Congress, been applied without intrenching upon the necessities of the Treasury, without adding a dollar to the taxes or debts of the community, without suspending even the steady and regular discharge of the debts contracted in former days, which within the same three years have been diminished by the amount of nearly $16,000,000.

The same observations are in a great degree applicable to the appropriations made for fortifications upon the coasts and harbors of the United States, for the maintenance of the Military Academy at West Point, and for the various objects under the superintendence of

the Department of the Navy. The report from the Secretary of the
Navy and those from the subordinate branches of both the military
departments exhibit to Congress in minute detail the present condition of the public establishment dependent upon them, the execution
of the acts of Congress relating to them, and the views of the officers engaged in the several branches of the service concerning the
improvements which may tend to their perfection. The fortification of
the coasts and the gradual increase and improvement of the Navy
are parts of a great system of national defense which has been upward of ten years in progress, and which for a series of years to
come will continue to claim the constant and persevering protection
and superintendence of the legislative authority. Among the measures
which have emanated from these principles the act of the last session
of Congress for the gradual improvement of the Navy holds a con-
spicuous place. The collection of timber for the future construction
of vessels of war, the preservation and reproduction of the species
of timber peculiarly adapted to that purpose, the construction of dry
docks for the use of the Navy, the erection of a marine railway for
the repair of the public ships, and the improvement of the navy-
yards for the preservation of the public property deposited in them
have all received from the Executive the attention required by that
act, and will continue to receive it, steadily proceeding toward the
execution of all its purposes. The establishment of a naval academy,
furnishing the means of theoretic instruction to the the youths who
devote their lives to the service of their country upon the ocean, still
solicits the sanction of the Legislature. Practical seamanship and the
art of navigation may be acquired on the cruises of the squadrons which
from time to time are dispatched to distant seas, but a competent
knowledge even of the art of shipbuilding, the higher mathematics,
and astronomy; the literature which can place our officers on a level
of polished education with the officers of other maritime nations; the
knowledge of the laws, municipal and national, which in their intercourse with foreign states and their governments are continually
called into operation, and above all, that acquaintance with the principles of honor and justice, with the higher obligations of morals and
of general laws, human and divine, which constitutes the great dis-
tinction between the warrior-patriot and the licensed robber and pri-
ate — these can be systematically taught and eminently acquired only
in a permanent school, stationed upon the shore and provided with
the teachers, the instruments, and the books conversant with and
adapted to the communication of the principles of these respective
sciences to the youthful and inquiring mind. . . .

Among the subjects which have heretofore occupied the earnest
solicitude and attention of Congress is the management and disposal
of that portion of the property of the nation which consists of the public lands. The acquistion of them, made at the expense of the whole
Union, not only in treasure but in blood, marks a right of property in

them equally extensive. By the report and statements from the General Land Office now communicated it appears that under the present Government of the United States a sum little short of $33,000,000 has been paid from the common Treasury for that portion of this property which has been purchased from France and Spain, and for the extinction of the aboriginal titles. The amount of lands acquired is near 260,000,000 acres, of which on the 1st of January, 1826, about 139,000,000 acres had been surveyed, and little more than 19,000,000 acres had been sold. The amount paid into the Treasury by the purchasers of the public lands sold is not yet equal to the sums paid for the whole, but leaves a small balance to be refunded. The proceeds of the sales of the lands have long been pledged to the creditors of the nation, a pledge from which we have reason to hope that they will in a very few years be redeemed.

The system upon which this great national interest has been managed was the result of long, anxious and persevering deliveration. Matured and modified by the progress of our population and the lessons of experience, it has been hitherto eminently successful. More than nine-tenths of the lands still remain the common property of the Union, the appropriation and disposal of which are sacred trusts in the hands of Congress. Of the lands sold, a considerable part were conveyed under extended credits, which in the vicissitudes and fluctuations in the value of lands and of their produce became oppressively burdensome to the purchasers. It can never be the interest or the policy of the nation to wring from its own citizens the reasonable profits of their industry and enterprise by holding them to the rigorous import of disastrous engagements. In March, 1821, a debt of $22,000,000, due by purchasers of the public lands, had accumulated which they were unable to pay. An act of Congress of the 2d March, 1821, came to their relief, and has been succeeded by others, the latest being the act of the 4th of May, 1826, the indulgent provisions of which expired on the 4th July last. The effect of these has been to reduce the debt from the purchasers to a remaining balance of about $4,300,000 due more than three-fifths of which are for lands within the State of Alabama. I recommend to Congress the revival and continuance for a further term of the beneficent accommodations to the public debtors of that statute, and submit to their consideration, in the same spirit of equity, the remission, under proper discriminations, of the forefeitures of partial payments on account of purchases of public lands, so far as to allow of their application to other payments.

There are various other subjects of deep interest to the whole Union which have heretofore been recommended to the consideration of Congress, as well by my predecessors as, under the impression of the duties devolving upon me, by myself. Among these are the debt, rather of justice than gratitude, to the surviving warriors of the Revolutionary war; the extension of the judicial administration of the Federal Government to those extensive and important members of the Union which, having risen into existence since the organization of the present judiciary establishment, now constitute at least one-third of its territory, power, and population; the formation of a more effective and uniform system for the government of the militia, and the amelioration in some form of modification of the diversified and often oppressive codes relating to insolvency. Amidst the multiplicity of topics of great national concernment which may recommend themselves to the calm and patriotic deliberations of the Legislature, it may suffice to say that on these and all other measures which may receive their sanction my hearty cooperation will be given, conformably to the duties enjoined upon me and under the sense of all the obligations prescribed by the Constitution.

## MESSAGE TO THE CONGRESS ON THE
## GEORGIA-CREEK INDIAN PROBLEM
### February 5, 1827

*When the Governor of Georgia refused to honor the Creek Indian Treaty. Adams threatened Federal Force. But in this message Adams, by referring the problem to Congress, deserted the Creeks. Congress failed to act, and finally another treaty, on November 15, 1827, gave Georgia all the Creek lands. Adams wanted more humane treatment for the Indians, but was unwilling to take the necessary risks involved in opposing "states rights."*

To the Senate and House of Representative of the United States:

I submit to the consideration of Congress a letter from the agent of the United States with the Creek Indians, who invoke the protection of the Government of the United States in defense of the rights and territory secured to that nation by the treaty concluded at Washington and ratified on the part of the United States on the 22nd of April last.

The compaint set forth in this letter that surveyors from Georgia have been employed in surveying lands within the Indian Territory, as secured by that treaty, is authenticated by the information inofficially received from other quarters, and there is reason to believe that one or more of the surveyors have been arrested in their progress by the Indians.

By the fifth section of the act of Congress of the 30th of March, 1802, to regulate trade and intercourse with the Indian tribes and to preserve peace on the frontiers, it is provided that if any citizen of or other person resident in the United States shall make a settlement on any lands belonging or secured or granted by treaty with the United States to any Indian tribe, or shall survey, or attempt to survey, such lands, or designate any of the boundaries by marking trees or otherwise, such offender shall forfeit a sum not exceeding $1,000 and suffer imprisionment not exceeding twelve months.

By the sixteenth and seventeenth sections of the same statute two distinct processes are prescribed, by either or both of which the above enactment may be carried into execution. By the first it is declared to be lawful for the military force of the United States to apprehend every person found in the Indian country over and beyond the boundary line between the United States and the Indian tribes in violation of any of the provisions or regulations of the act, and immediately to convey them in the nearest convenient and safe route, to the civil authority of the United States in some of the three next adjoining States or districts, to be proceeded against in due course of law.

By the second it is directed that if any person charged with the violation of any of the provisions or regulations of the act shall be found within any of the United States or either of their territorial districts such offender may be there apprehended and brought to trial in the same manner as if such crime or offense had been committed within such State or district and that it shall be the duty of the military force of the United States, when called upon by the civil magistrate or any proper officer or other person duly authorized for that purpose and having a lawful warrant, to aid and assist such magistrate, officer, or other person so authorized in arresting such offender and committing him to safe custody for trial according to law.

The first of these processes is adapted to the arrest of the trespasser upon Indian territories on the spot and in the act of committing the offense; but as it applies the action of the Government of the United States to places where civil process of the law has no authorized course, it is committed entirely to the functions of the military force to arrest the person of the offender, and after bringing him within the reach of the jurisdiction of the courts there to deliver him into custody for trial. The second makes the violator of the law amenable only after his offense has been consummated, and when he has returned within the civil jurisdiction of the Union. This process, in the first instance, is merely of a civil character, but may in like manner be enforced by calling in, if necessary, the aid of the military force. These modes of process, or to both, was within the discretion of the Executive authority, and penetrated with the duty of maintaining the rights of the Indians as secured both by the treaty and the law, concluded, after full deliberation to have recourse on this occasion, in the first instance, only to the civil process. Instructions have accordingly been given by the Secretary of War to the attorney and marshal of the United States in the district of Georgia to commence prosecutions against the surveyors complained of as having violated the law, while orders have at the same time been forwarded to the agent of the United States at once to assure the Indians that their rights founded upon the treaty and law are recognized by this Government and will be faithfully protected, and earnestly to exhort them, by the forbearance of every act of hostility on their part, to preserve unimpaired that right to protection secured by them by the sacred pledge of the good faith of this nation. Copies of these instructions and orders are herewith transmitted to Congress.

In abstaining at this stage of the proceedings from the application of any military force I have been governed by considerations which will, I trust, meet the concurrence of the Legislature. Among them one of paramount importance has been that these surveys have been attempted, and partly effected, under color of legal authority from the State of Georgia; that the surveyors are, therefore, not to be viewed in the light of individual and solitary transgressors, but as the agents of a sovereign State, acting in obedience to authority which they believe to be binding upon them. Intimations had been given that should they meet with interruption they would at all hazards be sustained by the military force of the State, in which event, if the military force of the Union should have been employed to enforce its violated, a conflict must have ensued, which would itself have inflicted a wound upon the Union and have presented the aspect of one of these confederated States at war with the rest. Anxious, above all, to avert this state of things, yet at the same time impressed with the deepest conviction of my own duty to take care that the laws shall be executed and the faith of the nation preserved I have used of the means intrusted to the Executive for that purpose only those which without resorting to military force may vindicate the sanctity of the law by the ordinary agency of the judicial tribunals.

It ought not, however, to be disguised that the act of the legislature of Georgia, under the construction given to it by the governor of that State, and the surveys made or attempted by his authority beyond the boundary secured by the treaty of Washington of April last to the Creek Indians, are in direct violation of the supreme law of this land set forth in a treaty which has received all the sanctions provided by the Constitution which we have been sworn to support and maintain.

Happily distributed as the sovereign powers of the people of this Union have been between their General and State Governments, their history has already too often presented collisions between these divided authorities with regard to the extent of their respective powers. No instance, however, has hitherto occurred in which this collision has been urged into a conflict of actual force. No other case is known to have happened in which the application of military force by the Government of the Union has been prescribed for the enforcement of a

law the violation of which has within any single State been prescribed
by a legislative act of the State. In the present instance it is my duty
to say that if the legislative and executive authorities of the State of
Georgia should persevere in acts of encroachment upon the territories secured by a solemn treaty to the Indians, and the laws of the
Union remain unaltered, a superadded obligation even higher than
that of human authority will compel the Executive of the United States
to enforce the laws and fulfill the duties of the nation by all the force
committed for that purpose to his charge. That the arm of military
force will be resorted to only in the event of the failure of all other
expedients provided by the laws, a pledge has been given by the forbearance to employ it at this time. It is submitted to the wisdom of
Congress to determine whether any further act of legislation may be
necessary or expedient to meet the emergency which these transactions may produce.

# FOURTH ANNUAL MESSAGE
## Washington, December 2, 1828

*Major portions of the fourth message deal with the prob-
lems of the British Trade which had been a thorn in his
side throughout his administration. Also important was
his plea for the revision of the Tariff of Nomination.*

Fellow-Citizens of the Senate and of the House of Representatives:

Of the enjoyment in profusion of the bounties of Providence forms
a suitable subject of mutual gratulation and grateful acknowledgment,
we are admonished at this return of the season when the representative of the nation are assembled to deliverate upon their concerns to
offer up the tribute of fervent and grateful hearts for the never-failing
mercies of Him who ruleth over all. He has again favored us with
healthful seasons and abundant harvests; He has sustained us in peace
with foreign countries and in tranquillity within our boarders; He has
preserved us in the quiet and undisturbed possession of civil and religious liberty; He has crowned the year with his goodness, imposing
on us no other conditions than of improving for our own happiness the

blessings bestowed by His hands, and, in the fruition of all His favors of devoting the faculties with which we have been endowed by Him to His glory and to our own temporal and eternal welfare.

In the relations of our Federal Union with our brethren of the human race the changes which have occurred since the close of your last session have generally tended to the preservation of peace and to the cultivation of harmony. Before your last separation a war had unhappily been kindled between the Empire of Russia, one of those with which our intercourse has been no other than a constant exchange of good offices and that of the Ottoman Porte, a nation from which geographical distance, religious opinions and maxims of government on their part little suited to the formation of those bonds of mutual benevolence which result from the benefits of commerce had kept us in a state, perhaps too much prolonged, of coldness and alienation. The extensive, fertile, and populous dominions of the Sultan belong rather to the Asiatic than the European division of the human family. They enter but partially into the system of Europe, nor have their wars with Russia and Austria, the European States upon which they border, for more than a century past disturbed the pacific relations of those States with the other great powers of Europe. Neither France nor Prussia nor Great Britain has ever taken part in them, nor is it to be expected that they will at this time. The declaration of war by Russia has received the approbation or acquiescence of her allies, and we may indulge the hope that its progress and termination will be signalized by the moderation and forbearance no less than by the energy of the Emperor Nicholas, and that it will afford the opportunity for such collateral agency in behalf of the suffering Greeks as will secure to them ultimately the triumph of humanity and of freedom.

The state of our particular relations with France has scarcely varied in the course of the present year. The commercial intercourse between the two countries has continued to increase for the mutual benefit of both. The claims of indemnity to numbers of our fellow-citizens for depredations upon their property, heretofore committed during the revolutionary governments, remain unadjusted, and still form the subject of earnest representation and remonstrance. Recent advices from the minister of the United States at Paris encourage the expectation that the appeal to the justice of the French Government will ere long receive a favorable consideration.

The last friendly expedient has been resorted to for the decision of the controversy with Great Britain relating to the northeastern boundary of the United States. By an agreement with the British Government, carrying into effect the provisions of the fifth article of the treaty of Ghent, and the convention of 29th September, 1827, His Majesty the King of Netherlands has by common consent been selected as the umpire between the parties. The proposal to him to accept the designation for the performance of this friendly office will be made at an early day and the United States, relying upon the justice of their cause, will cheerfully commit the arbitrament of it to a prince equally distinguished for the independence of his spirit, his indefatigable assiduity to the duties of his station, and his inflexible personal probity.

Our commercial relations with Great Britain will deserve the serious considerations of Congress and the exercise of a conciliatory and forbearing spirit in the policy of both Governments. The state of them has been materially changed by the act of Congress, passed at their last session, in alteration of the several acts imposing duties on imports, and by act of more recent date of the British Parliament. The effect of the interdiction of direct trade, commenced by Great Britain and reciprocated by the United States, has been, as was to be foreseen, only to substitute different channels for an exchange of commodities indispensable to the colonies and profitable to a numerous class of our fellow-citizens. The exports. the revenue, the navigation of the United States have suffered no diminution by our exclusion from direct access to the British colonies. The colonies pay more dearly for the necessaries of life which their Government burdens with the charges of double voyages, freight insurance, and commission, and the profits of our exports are somewhat impaired and more injuriously transferred from one portion of our citizens to another. The resumption of this old and otherwise exploded system of colonial exclusion has not secured to the shipping interest of Great Britain the relief which, at the expense of the distant colonies and of the United States, it was expected to afford. Other measures have been resorted to more pointedly bearing upon the navigation of the United States, and which, unless modified by the construction given to the recent acts of Parliament, will be manifestly incompatible with the positive stipulations of the commercial convention existing between the two countries. That convention, however, may be terminated with twelve months' notice, at the option of either party....

Immediately after the close of the War of Independence commissioners were appointed by the Congress of the Confederation authorized to conclude treaties with every nation of Europe disposed to adopt them. Before the wars of the French Revolution such treaties had been consummated with the United Netherlands, Sweden, and Prussia. During those wars treaties with Great Britain and Spain had been effected, and those with Prussia and France renewed. In all these some concessions to the liberal principles of intercourse proposed by the United States had been obtained; but as in all the negotiations they came occasionally in collision with previous internal regulations or exclusive and excluding compacts of monopoly with which the other parties had been trammeled, the advances made in them toward the freedom of trade were partial and imperfect. Colonial establishments, chartered companies, and shipbuilding influence pervaded and encumbered the legislation of all the great commercial states; and the

United States, in offering free trade and privilege to all were com-
pelled to acquiesce in many exceptions with each of the parties to
their treaties, accommodated to their existing laws and anterior
engagements.

The colonial system by which this whole hemisphere was bound
has fallen into ruins, totally abolished by revolutions converting colonies into independent nations throughout the two American continents, excepting a portion of territory chiefly at the northern extremity
of our own, and confined to the remnants of dominion retained by
Great Britain over the insular archipelago, geographically the append-
ages of our part of the globe. With all the rest we have free trade,
even with the insular colonies of all the European nations, except
Great Britain. Her Government also had manifested approaches to
the adoption of a free and liberal intercourse between her colonies and
other nations, though by a sudden and scarcely explained revulsion the
spirit of exclusion has been revived for operation upon the United
States alone.

The conclusion of our last treaty of peace with Great Britain was
shortly afterwards followed by a commercial convention, placing the
direct intercourse between the two countries upon a footing of more
equal reciprocity than had ever before been admitted. The same principle has since been much further extended by treaties with France,
Sweden, Denmark, the Hanseatic cities, Prussia, in Europe, and with
the mutual abolition of discriminating duties and charges upon the
navigation and commercial intercourse between the parties is the
general maxim which characterizes them all. There is reason to ex-
pect that it will at no distant period be adopted by other nations, both
of Europe and America, and to hope that by its universal prevalence
one of the fruitful sources of wars of commercial competition will be
extinguished. . . .

The great interest of an agricultural, commercial and manufacturing nation are so linked in union together that no permanent cause of
prosperity to one of them can operate without extending its influence to
the others. All these interests are alike under the protecting power
of the legislative authority, and the duties of the representative bodies
are to conciliate them in harmony together. So far as the object of
taxation is to raise a revenue for discharging the debts and defraying
the expenses of the community, its operation should be adapted as
much as possible to suit the burden with equal hand upon all proportion with their ability of bearing it without oppression. But the legislation of one nation is sometimes intentionally made to bear heavily
upon the interests of another. That legislation, adapted, as it is meant
to be, to the special interests of its own people, will often press most
unequally upon the several component interests of its neighbors.
Thus the legislation of Great Britain, when, as has recently been
avowed, adapted to the depression of a rival nation, will naturally

abound with regulations of interdict upon the productions of the soil or industry of the other which come in competition with its own, and will present encouragement, perhaps even bounty, to the raw material of the other State which it can not produce itself, and which is essential for the use of its manufactures, competitors in the markets of the world with those of its commercial rival. Such is the state of the commercial legislation of Great Britain as it bears upon our interests. It excludes with interdicting duties all importation (except in time of approaching famine) of the great staple of productions of our Middle and Western States; it proscribes with equal rigor our bulkier lumber and live stock of the same portion and also of the Northern and Eastern part of our Union. It refuses even the rice of the South unless aggravated with a charge of duty upon the Northern carrier who brings it to them. But the cotton, indispensable for their looms, they will receive almost duty free to weave it into a fabric for our own wear, to the destruction of our own manufactures, which they are enabled thus to undersell.

Is the self-protecting energy of this nation so helpless that there exists in the political institutions of our country no power to counteract the bias of this foreign legislation; that the growers of grain must submit to this exclusion from the foreign markets of their produce; that the shippers must dismantle their ships, the trade of the North stagnate at the wharves, and the manufacturers starve at their looms, while the whole people shall pay tribute to foreign industry to be clad in a foreign garb; that the Congress of the Union are impotent to restore the balance in favor of native industry destroyed by the statutes of another realm? More just and more generous sentiments will, I trust, prevail. If the tariff adopted at the last session of Congress shall be found by experience to bear oppressively upon the interests of any one section of the Union, it ought to be, and I can not doubt will be, so modified as to alleviate its burden. To the voice of just complaint from any portion of the constituents, the representatives of the States and of the people will never turn away their ears. But so long as the duty of the foreign shall operate only as a bounty upon the domestic article; while the planter and the merchant and the shepherd and the husbandman shall be found thriving in their occupations under the duties imposed for the protection of domestic manufacturers, they will not repine at the prospertity shared with themselves by their fellow-citizens of other professions, nor denounce as violations of the Constitution the deliberate acts of Congress to shield from the wrongs of foreign laws the native industry of the Union. While the tariff of the last session of Congress was a subject of legislative deliberation it was foretold by some of its opposers that one of its necessary consequences would be to impair the revenue. It is yet too soon to pronounce with confidence that this prediction was erroneous. The obstruction of one avenue of trade not unfrequently opens an issue to another. The consequence of the tariff will be to increase the exportation and to diminish the importation of others, the duties upon which will supply the deficiencies which the diminished importation would otherwise occasion. The effect of taxation upon revenue can seldom be foreseen with certainty. It must abide the test of experience. As yet no symptoms of diminution are perceptible in the receipts of the Treasury. As yet little addition of cost has even been experienced upon the articles burdened with heavier duties by the last tariff. The domestic manufacturer supplies the same or a kindred article at a diminished price, and the consumer pays the same tribute to the labor of his own countryman which he must otherwise have paid to foreign industry and toil.

The tariff of the last session was in its details not acceptable to the great interests of any portion of the Union, not even to the interest which it was specially intended to subserve. Its object was to balance the burdens upon native industry imposed by the operation of foreign laws, but not to aggravate the burdens of one section of the Union by the relief afforded to another. To the great principle sanctioned by that act – one of those upon which the Constitution itself was formed – I hope and trust the authorities of the Union will adhere. But if any of the duties imposed by the act only relieve the manufacturer by aggravating the burden of the planter, let a careful revisal of its provisions, enlightened by the practical experience of its effects, be directed to retain those which impart protection to native industry and remove or supply the place of those which only alleviate one great national interest by the depression of another.

The United States of America and the people of every State of which they are composed are each of them sovereign powers. The legislative authority of the whole is exercised by Congress under authority granted them in the common Constitution. The legislative power of each State is exercised by assemblies deriving their authority from the constitution of the State. Each is sovereign within its own province. The distribution of power between them presupposes that these authorities will move in harmony with each other. The members of the State and General Governments are, all under oath to support both, and allegiance is due to the one and to the other. The case of a conflict between these two powers has not been supposed, nor has any provision been made for it in our institutions; as a virtuous nation of ancient times existed more than five centuries without a law for the punishment of parricide.

More than once, however, in the progress of our history have the people and the legislatures of one or more States, in moments of excitement been instigated to this conflict; and the means of effecting this impulse have been allegations that the acts of Congress to be resisted were unconstitutional. The people of no one State have ever delegated to their legislature the power of pronouncing an act of Congress unconstitutional, but they have delegated to them powers by the exercise of which the execution of the laws of Congress within the State may be resisted. If we suppose the case of such conflicting legislation sustained by the corresponding executive and judicial authorities, patriotism and philanthropy turn their eyes from the condition in which the parties would be placed, and from that of the people of both, which must be its victims. . . .

The attention of Congress is particularly invited to that part of the report of the Secretary of War which concerns the existing system of our relations with the Indian tribes. At the establishment of the Federal Government under the present Constitution of the United States the principle was adopted of considering them as foreign and independent powers and also as proprietors of lands. They were, moreover, considered as savages, whom it was our policy and our duty to use our influence in converting to Christianity and in bringing within the pale of civilization.

As independent powers, we negotiated with them by treaties; as proprietors, we purchased of them all the lands which we could prevail upon them to sell; as brethern of the human race, rude and ignorant, endeavored to bring them to the knowledge of religion and letters. The ultimate design was to incorporate in our own institutions that portion of them which could be converted to the state of civilization. In the practice of European States, before our Revolution, they had been considered as children to be governed; as tenants at discretion, to be dispossessed as occasion might require; as hunters to be indemnified by trifling concessions for removal from the grounds from which their game was extirpated. In changing the system it would seem as if a full contemplation of the consequences of the change had not been taken. We have been far more successful in the acquisition of their lands than in imparting to them the principles or inspiring them with the spirit of civilization. But in appropriating to ourselves their hunting grounds we have brought upon ourselves the obligation of providing them with subsistence; and when we have had the rare good fortune of teaching them the arts of civilization and the doctrines of Christianity we have unexpectedly found them forming in the midst of ourselves communities claiming to be independent of ours and rivals of sovereignty within the territories of the members of our Union. This state of things requires that a remedy should be provided — a remedy which, while it shall do justice to those unfortunate children of nature, may secure to the members of our confederation their rights of sovereignty and of soil. As the outline of a project to that effect, the views presented in the report of the Secretary of War are recommended to the consideration of Congress.

The report from the Engineer Department presents a comprehensive view of the progress which has been made in the great systems promotive of the public interest, commenced and organized under authority of Congress, and the effects of which have already contributed to the security, as they will hereafter largely contribute to the honor and dignity, of the nation.

The first of these great systems is that of fortifications, commended immediately after the close of our last war, under the salutary experience which the events of that war had impressed upon our countrymen of its necessity. Introduced under the auspices of my immediate predecessor it has been continued with the presevering and liberal encouragement of the Legislature, and, combined with corresponding exertions for the gradual increase and improvement of the Navy, prepare for our extensive country a condition of defense adapted to any critical emergency which the varying course of events may bring forth. Our advances in these concerted systems have for the last ten years been steady and progressive and in a few years more will be so completed as to leave no cause for apprehension that our seacoast will ever again offer a theater of hostile invasion.

The next of these cardinal measures of policy is the preliminary to great and lasting works of public improvement in the surveys of roads, examination for the course of canals, and labors for the removal of the obstructions of rivers and harbors, first commenced by the act of Congress of 30th April, 1824.

The report exhibits in one table the funds appropriated at the last and preceding sessions of Congress for all these fortifications, surveys, and works of public improvement, the manner in which these funds have been applied, the amount expended upon the several works under construction and the further sums which may be necessary to complete them; in a second the works projected by the Board of Engineers which have not been commenced and the estimate of their cost; in a third, the report of the annual Board of Visitors at the Military Academy at West Point.

For thirteen fortifications erecting on various points of our Atlantic coast, from Rhode Island to Louisiana, the aggregate expenditure of the year has fallen little short of $1,000,000. For the preparation of five additional reports of reconnaissances and surveys since the last session of Congress, for the civil constructions upon thirty-seven different public works commenced, eight others for which specific appropriations have been made by acts of Congress and twenty other incipient surveys under the authority given by the act of 30th April, 1824, about one million more of dollars has been drawn from the Treasury.

To these $2,000,000 is to be added the appropriation of $250,000 to commence the erection of a breakwater near the mouth of the Delaware River, the subscriptions to the Delaware and Chesapeake, the Louisville and Portland, the Dismal Swamp, and the Chesapeake and Ohio canals, the large donations of lands to the States of Ohio, Indiana, Illinois, and Alabama for objects of improvements within those

States, and the sums appropriated for light-houses, buoys, and piers on the coast; and a full view will be taken of the munificence of the nation in the application of its resources to the improvement of its own condition. . . .

A resolution of the House of Representatives requesting that one of our small public vessels should be sent to the Pacific Ocean and South Sea to examine the coasts, islands, harbors, shoals, and reefs in those seas, and to ascertain their true situation and description, has been put in a train of execution. The vessel is nearly ready to depart. The successful accomplishment of the expedition may be greatly facilitated by suitable legislative provisions, and particularly by an appropriation to defray its necessary expense. The addition of a second, and perhaps a third, vessel, with a slight aggravation of the cost, would contribute much to the safety of the citizens embarked on this undertaking, the results of which may be of the deepest interest to our country. . . .

Among the important subjects to which the attention of the present Congress has already been invited, and which may occupy their further and deliberate discussion, will be the provision to be made for taking the fifth census or enumeration of the inhabitants of the United States. The Constitution of the United States requires that this enumeration should be made within every term of ten years, and the date from which the last enumeration commenced was the first Monday of August of the year 1820. The laws under which the former enumerations were taken were enacted at the session of Congress immediately preceding the operation; but considerable inconveniences were experienced from the delay of legislation to so late a period. That law, like those of the preceding enumerations, directed that the cenus should be taken by the marshals of the several districts and Territories of the Union under instructions from the Secretary of State. The preparation and transmission to the marshals of those instructions required more time than was then allowed between the passage of the law and the day when the enumeration was to commence. Their term of six months limited for the returns of the marshals was also found even then too short, and must be more so now, when an additional population of at 3,000,000 must be presented upon the returns. As they are to be made at the short session of Congress, it would, as well as from other considerations, be more convenient to commence the enumeration from an earlier period of the year than the 1st of August. The most favorable season would be the spring. On a review of the former enumerations it will be found that the plan for taking every census has contained many improvements upon that of its predecessor. The last is still susceptible of much improvement. The Third Census was the first at which any account was taken of the manufactures of the country. It was repeated at the last enumeration, but the returns in both cases were necessarily very imperfect. They must always be so, resting, of course, only upon the communications voluntarily made by individuals interested in some of the manufacturing establishments. Yet they contained much valuable information, and may be by some supplementary provision of the law be rendered more effective. The columns of age, commencing from infancy, have hitherto been confined to a few periods, all under the number of 45 years. Important knowledge would be obtained by extending these columns, in intervals of ten years, to the utmost boundaries of human life. The labor of taking them would be a trifling addition to that already prescribed, and the result would exhibit comparative tables of longevity highly interesting to the country. I deem it my duty further to observe that much of the imperfections in the returns of the last and perhaps of preceding enumerations proceeded from the inadequateness of the compensations allowed to the marshals and their assistants in taking them.

In closing this communication it only remains for me to assure the Legislature of my continued earnest wish for the adoption of measures recommended by me heretofore and yet to be acted on by them, and of the cordial concurrence on my part in every constitutional provision which may receive their sanction during the session tending to the general welfare.

## DIARY ENTRY AFTER THE GAG RULE WAS REVOKED
### December 3, 1844

*Adams' greatest fight as a congressman concerned the revoking of the gag rule. For eight years he labored to repress it and in so doing, became a center for the anti-slavery forces.*

December 3, 1844... In pursuance of the notice I had given yesterday, I moved the following resolution: "Resolved, that the twenty-fifth standing rule for conducting business in this House, in the following words, No petition, memorial, resolution, or other paper praying the abolition of slavery in the District of Columbia or any State or Territory, or the slave trade between the States or Territories in which it now exists, shall be received by this House, or entertained in any way whatever,' be, and the same is, hereby rescinded." I called for the yeas and nays. Jacob Thompson of Mississippi moved to lay the resolution on the table I called for the yeas and nays on that motion. As the clerk was about to begin the call, the President's message was announced and received. A member called for the reading of the message. I said I hoped the question upon my resolution would be taken. The clerk called the roll, and the motion to lay on the table was rejected — 81 to 104. The question was then put on the resolution; and it was carried — 108 to 80. Blessed, forever blessed, be the name of God!

# BIBLIOGRAPHICAL AIDS

# BIBLIOGRAPHICAL AIDS

The emphasis in this and other volumes in the Presidential Chronologies series is on the administrations of the Presidents. The more important works on other aspects of their lives, before and after their terms, are included since they contribute to an understanding of the presidential careers. Holding these aspects down to size is especially difficult for John Quincy Adams; a rather disappointing Administration was surrounded by two brilliant careers — the diplomat and the congressman.

The following bibliography is critically selected and contains works, for the most part, which are readily available to students. Listing out of print books that would be almost impossible to find seemed to offer little value, unless the work was critical to the life of the man. Additional titles may be found in the Harvard Guide to American History, Cambridge, 1954. For recent articles in scholarly journals, consult the Reader's Guide to Periodical Literature and the Social Sciences and Humanities Index.

# SOURCE MATERIALS

Since John Quincy Adams was a prolific writer, a great amount of material has been published, but a great amount of material still remains unpublished. Perhaps the best source for the really serious student would be the complete microfilm edition of his papers which is available from the Massachusetts Historical Society.

Adams, Charles F. Memoirs of John Qunicy Adams, Comprising Part of His Diary from 1775 to 1848. 12 vol. Philadelphia, 1875-77. A good accurate source for dates and events, but colored by Adams' strong point of view. Just how much a son's editing may have affected his father's image is difficult to estimate.

Ford, William C., ed. The Writings of John Quincy Adams. 7 vol. New York, 1913-17. Volumes stop at 1823, thus offers no information for the presidential years.

Israel, Fred L., ed. The State of the Union Messages of the Presidents, with an introduction by Arthur M. Schlesinger New York, 1967.

Kock, Adrienne & Peden, William, ed. The Selected Writings of John and John Quincy Adams. New York, 1946. Interestingly condensed in one volume.

Nevins, Allan. The Diary of John Quincy Adams, 1794-1845. New York, 1928. Good, but just too much material for a one volume work.

Richardson, James D. A Compilation of the Messages and Papers of the Presidents. Vol. II. Washington, 1897. Standard source from which the state documents in this volume have been taken.

## BIOGRAPHIES

Adams, James Truslow. The Adams Family. New York, 1930. Interesting but lacking in specific dates. John Quincy Adams is covered in vol. 11.

Bemis, Samuel Flagg. John Quincy Adams and the Foundations of American Foreign Policy. New York, 1949.

Bemis, Samuel Flagg. John Quincy Adams and the Union. New York, 1956. The two Bemis' volumes are considered the standard biography. The first book covers Adams' boyhood and diplomatic career. The second book covers the presidency and the years in the House of Representatives. Quite factual, and for the first time the biographer had complete access to all the Adams papers. Misses only in not presenting a full personality of the man.

Bobbe, Dorothie. Mr. & Mrs. John Quincy Adams. New York. 1930. Quaint and dull.

Clark, Bennett Champ. John Quincy Adams, "Old Man Elequent." Boston, 1933. Attempts to portray the congressman.

Falkner, Leonard. The President Who Wouldn't Retire. New York, 1967. A good factual handling of Adams' later career in the House.

Lipsky, George A. John Quincy Adams, His Theory and Ideas. New York, 1950. Interesting, but lacking in specifics.

Seward, William H. Life and Public Services of John Quincy Adams. New York, 1849. Earliest biography by a contemporary. Highly slanted.

Steinberg, Alfred. The First Ten. New York, 1967. Gives a short but good picture of Adams' Administration.

## ESSAYS

Bemis, Samuel F. "John Quincy Adams and Russia," Virginia Quarterly Review, v. XXI. (October, 1945), 553-68.

"Mad Old Man from Mass.," American Heritage, LXXII. (April, 1961), 64-71.

Perkins, Dexter. "John Quincy Adams," in American Secretaries of State, edited by Samuel Flagg Bemis (New York, 1928), IV, 1-111.

Sydor, Charles S. "The One-Party Period of American History," American Historical Review, LI. (April, 1946), 439-51.

## MONOGRAPHS AND SPECIAL AREAS

Barnes, Gilbert H. The Antislavery Impulse, 1830-1844. New York, 1933. Offers excellent coverage of Adams' gag rule fight.

Dangerfield, George. The Awakening of American Nationalism, 1815-1828. New York, 1965.

Dangerfield, George. The Era of Good Feelings. New York, 1952. Both of Dangerfield's books offer a solid background for the general period, and good coverage of the Adams' Administration.

Dos Passos, John. The Shackles of Power, Three Jeffersonian Decades. New York, 1966. A good look at the general period.

Ownes, William A. Slave Mutiny: The Revolt on the Schooner Amistad. New York, 1953.

Perkins, Dexter. The Monroe Doctrine, 1823-1826. Cambridge, Mass., 1927. The standard work.

Schlesinger, Arthur M., Jr. The Age of Jackson. Boston, 1945.
    Good for the social and political aspects of the times.

Stanwood, Edward. American Tarrif Controversies in the Nineteenth
    Century. Boston & New York, 1903. Excellent coverage of the
    tariff of abominations.

Whitaker, Arthur Preston. The United States and the Independence of
    Latin America. Baltimore, 1941.

Wiltse, Charles M. John C. Calhoun, Nationalist, 1782-1828. Indianap-
    olis & New York, 1944.

Wiltse, Charles M. John C. Calhoun, Nullifier, 1829-1839. Indianapolis
    & New York, 1949.

Wiltse, Charles M. John C. Calhoun, Sectionalist, 1840-1853. Indianap-
    olis & New York, 1951. Wiltse's three Calhoun books are con-
    sidered by many experts as presenting the best picture of
    the age. Coverage of Adams' administration is especially good.

## THE PRESIDENCY

Bailey, Thomas A. Presidential Greatness The Image and the Man
    from George Washington to the Present. Forty-three yard-
    sticks for measuring presidential ability. He places John
    Quincy Adams on the low end of the "high average" group.
    An interesting presentation with little practical value except
    for the bibliography.

Brinkley, Wilfred E. The Man in the White House His Powers and
    Duties. Revised ed. New York, 1965. Good history of the growth
    of the president's powers.

Corwin, Edward S. The President Office and Powers. New York, 1957.

Kane, Joseph Nathan. Facts About the Presidents. New York, 1959.
    Good biographical information.

Koenig, Louis W. The Chief Executive. New York, 1964. Highly useful.

Laski, Harold J. The American Presidency. New York, 1940. A precise defining of the presidential powers.

Rossiter, Clinton. The American Presidency. Second Ed. New York, 1960.

# NAME INDEX

Adams, Abigail Brooks, daughter in law, 17
Adams, Abigail Smith, mother, 1, 8, 20
Adams, Charles, brother, 1, 2, 3, 4
Adams, Charles Francis, son, 6, 17, 20
Adams, George Washington, son, 4, 17
Adams, Henry, grandson, 18
Adams, John, father, 1, 4, 5, 12, 13, 20
Adams, John II, son, 5, 15, 17, 18
Adams, John Q. II, grandson, 18
Adams, Louisa Catherine Johnson, wife, 4, 6, 20
Adams, Louisa Catherine granddaughter, 17
Adams, Mary Helen, daughter in law, 15, 17
Adams, Mary Louisa, granddaughter 16, 17
Adam, Thomas, brother, 4
Ames, Fisher, 6
Anderson, Richard C., 12, 13

Barbour, James, 11, 14
Bayard, James, 7
Brooks, Peter, 17
Brown, James, 11

Calhoun, John C., 10, 11, 13, 14, 16
Castlereagh, Lord, 7
Catherine, the Great, 2
Clay, Henry, 7, 10, 11, 13, 16
Crawford, William, 10, 11

Dana, Francis, 2
Davis, John, 17, 18

Everett, Alexander, 11

Franklin, Benjamin, 1, 2

Gallatin, Albert, 7, 13
Genet, Citizen, 3
Green, Duff, 12

Hughes, Christopher, 11

Jackson, Andrew, 7, 8, 10, 15, 16
Jackson, Rachel, 16
Jarvis, Russell, 15
Jay, John, 2, 3, 4
Jefferson, Thomas, 3, 4, 6, 13, 16
Johnson, Joshua, 4

King, Rufus, 11, 13

Lee, Arthur, 1
Letcher, Robert, 10
Lloyd, James, 6

Madison, James, 6
McLean, James, 11
Monroe, James, 7, 8, 9, 10
Mott, Martin V., 14

Napoleon, 7

Paine, Thomas, 3
Parsons, Theophilus, 2
Poinsett, Joel, 11
Porter, David, 16
Porter, Peter, 11

Randolph, Edmund, 3
Randolph, John, 13
Richardson, Joseph, 17
Rodney, Caesar A., 9
Rush, Richard, 11, 16
Russell, John, 7

Sergeant, John 12, 13
Smithson, James, 18

# TITLES IN THE OCEANA
# PRESIDENTIAL CHRONOLOGY SERIES
Reference books containing
Chronology—Documents—Bibliographical Aids
for each President covered.
*Series Editor:* **Howard F. Bremer**

**GEORGE WASHINGTON***
*edited by* Howard F. Bremer

**JOHN ADAMS***
*edited by* Howard F. Bremer

**JAMES BUCHANAN***
*edited by* Irving J. Sloan

**GROVER CLEVELAND****
*edited by* Robert I. Vexler

**FRANKLIN PIERCE***
*edited by* Irving J. Sloan

**ULYSSES S. GRANT****
*edited by* Philip R. Moran

**MARTIN VAN BUREN****
*edited by* Irving J. Sloan

**THEODORE ROOSEVELT****
*edited by* Gilbert Black

**BENJAMIN HARRISON***
*edited by* Harry J. Sievers

**JAMES MONROE***
*edited by* Ian Elliot

**WOODROW WILSON****
*edited by* Robert I. Vexler

**RUTHERFORD B. HAYES***
*edited by* Arthur Bishop

**ANDREW JACKSON****
*edited by* Ronald Shaw

**JAMES MADISON****
*edited by* Ian Elliot

**HARRY S TRUMAN*****
*edited by* Howard B. Furer

**WARREN HARDING****
*edited by* Philip Moran

**DWIGHT D. EISENHOWER*****
*edited by* Robert I. Vexler

**JAMES K. POLK***
*edited by* John J. Farrell

**JOHN QUINCY ADAMS***
*edited by* Kenneth Jones

**HARRISON/TYLER*****
*edited by* David A. Durfee

**ABRAHAM LINCOLN*****
*edited by* Ian Elliot

**GARFIELD/ARTHUR*****
*edited by* Howard B. Furer

*Available Soon*

**WILLIAM McKINLEY**
*edited by* Harry J. Sievers

**ANDREW JOHNSON**
*edited by* John N. Dickinson

**WILLIAM HOWARD TAFT**
*edited by* Gilbert Black

**JOHN F. KENNEDY**
*edited by* Ralph A. Stone

**THOMAS JEFFERSON**
*edited by* Arthur Bishop

**TAYLOR/FILLMORE**
*edited by* John J. Farrell

**CALVIN COOLIDGE**
*edited by* Philip Moran

**LYNDON B. JOHNSON**
*edited by* Howard B. Furer

**FRANKLIN D. ROOSEVELT**
*edited by* Howard F. Bremer

**HERBERT HOOVER**
*edited by* Arnold Rice

\*    96 pages, $3.00/B
\*\*  128 pages, $4.00/B
\*\*\* 160 pages, $5.00/B